Ghostly Tales From America's Jails

Edited by
Joan Upton Hall

ISBN
1-933177-09-8 (10 digit)
978-1-933177-09-0 (13 digit)

Library of Congress Control Number 2006935617

First Edition

Printed in the United States of America
Published by Atriad Press LLC
13820 Methuen Green
Dallas, TX 75240
(972) 671-0002
FAX (214) 367-4398
www.atriadpress.com

Acknowledgements

The editor wishes to thank the many who have contributed to this book: people (living and deceased) who lived the stories, authors researching and writing the stories, organizations that manage the facilities, and various individuals who shared their information and photographs.

Special appreciation goes to Janet and Bryan Kilgore for collecting the photographs.

Table of Contents

Call them hoosegows, calabooses, or correctional institutions—by the very nature of old jails and prisons, misery and violent events took place there. No wonder a few sundry ghosts have lingered: prisoners destined to keep existing in misery or guards who never get to retire.

Let us share haunting stories told by people who have experienced them—from either side of the bars. Museum curators, tour guides, correctional officers, prisoners, and even visitors encounter sounds, scents, sights, and tactile sensations that chill them to the marrow. Investigators of the paranormal seek verification by way of film, thermal readings, heart rates, and electronic voice phenomena, but as they say, "To a believer, no proof is necessary. To a disbeliever, no proof is enough." – Derk Acorah, quoted on several ghost hunter sites.

For ghost hunters, the types of hauntings can be classified and studied. But for casual observers, like me, any kind of ghost gives us the willies.

The chapters are arranged in chronological order from the oldest to the youngest haunted jail. Follow this facet of America's history while you read tales that'll make you check the locks on your doors and pull up a warm cat or two.

Few old jails still house lawbreakers today because they don't meet modern standards for incarceration. But these remarkable old structures are too good to tear down and too full of history—and hauntings—to forget. Some have been transformed into restaurants, inns, offices, or shops. Many are museums that remind visitors of the inhumane conditions prisoners were once subjected to. It may appall you to read that some of the methods of punishment started off as attempts to turn heinous prisoners into nice folks.

Solitary confinement was a chief example. The entire building design of Pennsylvania's 1829 Penitentiary furnished "an experiment in solitude," complete and everyday. Almost all prisons had what they called "the hole." At least it was temporary, but varied in the sort of "amenities" provided.

Some methods were almost certainly conceived out of the sadism of those in charge—such as the way solitary was administered at Charleston, South Carolina's 1802 Old City Jail. Heaven help the poor ghosts sentenced to eternity there.

Jail museums display artifacts of an earlier time when the required method of execution was by hanging and later the electric chair, affectionately known as "Old Sparky." Other exhibits show how prisoners failed or succeeded at jail breaks: a fatal miscalculation at the 1880 Folsom Prison, and the truly desperate attempt considering the stuff some POWs swam through at the 1859 Fort Delaware Prison. A few prisoners simply disappeared—and still reappear from time to time. Some jails used ingenious devices to "escape-proof" their facility, such as the rotary cells at the 1885 "Squirrel Cage" in Iowa.

Read about the lengths executioners were expected to go to in providing a "proper" death for the condemned, such as the engineering that went into an effective gallows, not to mention the punishment the hangman might face if he did it wrong, delivering a slow death to the hapless the victim. Slow death was not a concern to the executioner if the prisoner had been sentenced to being "pressed" to death at the 1684 Witch Jail in Massachusetts.

Facts about the jail buildings, along with interesting events and people connected with them give you a taste of what it must have been like if your address was one of these "home sweet hoosegows." Surprisingly, not all the ghosts were miserable, and may be staying by choice, as in the 1872 Wyoming Prison. Actually some ghosts seem to think they're employees—if not owners—of whatever business has found new digs in an old jail. At the 1872 jail, turned B&B, in Arkansas, the long-deceased sheriff checks the locks for his guests—or does he think they're prisoners?

Addresses and contact information of the institutions will make it easy for you to visit the sites—if you dare. Several of the institutions in this book may look familiar. Check out which movies have been filmed at these places in modern times. A high-profile case recounted in the 1834 New York chapter inspired not only a best-selling novel and movie but an opera as well.

Contributing authors for this book range from ghost hunters, to psychics, to correctional officers, to—perhaps your next-door-neighbor, who was just visiting a certain site. You'll find not only multi-published authors but also those making their debut in print. Don't miss the writer's bio at the end of each chapter.

And don't miss the creative names for ghost-hunting organizations and tour names mentioned throughout the book. I am especially indebted to these experts.

Have a haunting good time with what we've dug up for you!

Photo by Daryl Black

The Palace Ghosts - 1610

The Palace of Governors, Santa Fe, NM

by Robert Jesten Upton

The Palace of Governors was the terminus for the Camino Real—the Royal Road—that led north from Mexico, which was the most remote reach of the Spanish Empire, and it was the magnet that drew traders, travelers, and pioneers from the east down the Santa Fe Trail. It was already ten years old when the Pilgrims set foot on Plymouth Rock.

In the four centuries since Santa Fe, New Mexico, was founded, the city has accumulated its share of "restless spirits." La Llorona wails down its old streets and alleyways, searching for her drowned children, a well-known ghost from the Spanish tradition. Hardly a building in the old city is without a haunt or two. Even newer buildings like the one where I work, the Garrey Carruthers State Library, have their "presences." Ours is familiar with the people who work in a particular part of the building on the ground floor, calling us by our names in otherwise deserted hallways.

At first it made no sense to me how a new building could have an old spirit until I recalled that the new structure was built on the site of the old Army Hospital from WWII where many souls passed from this side into the next—or failed in some cases to make the full transition. Then I understood our invisible colleague, and appreciated the benign familiarity so singularly expressed.

Of all the homes, offices, warehouses, et cetera, in Santa Fe that local tradition holds to be "spooked," surely the oldest site has had the greatest opportunity for trapping lost souls: the Palace of the Governors.

First constructed in 1609-10 by the Spanish Governor Don Pedro de Peralta, at one time under the flag of Spain, all the lands west of the Mississippi were governed from the Palace of the Governors. Rebellious Indians took it in 1680, but by 1692 De Vargas won it back. The Palace has housed 90 governors from three nations as well as territorial governors, one of whom, Lew Wallace, wrote Ben Hur while in office (novel published in 1880). During the Civil War, the Palace flew the Confederate flag for two weeks before the Union troops took over.

It has been inhabited by conquistadors, Spanish colonists, garrisoned soldiers, rebelling Indians, Mexican commandants, mountain men, and a daily flow of citizens and visitors. The often-remodeled and continuously inhabited building has been a cornerstone to the settlement of the Western United States.

The "Adobe Palace" was built as part of the Spanish presidio or garrison and extended 350 feet along the north side of the city plaza. It has housed various governors, the legislative assembly, legal courts, government offices, a library, a bakery, and a bank; it has served as garrison, armory, depository, post office, and... a jail.

The jail occupied the west end of the Palace, at what is now the corner of Palace and Lincoln Avenues, from the mid 1700s until at least 1846 when the American army marched into the newly incorporated territory after the Mexican War. Use as a prison may have lasted longer, for local legend has it that the bars still in place in the windows facing Lincoln Avenue were recycled from Confederate supplies.

Tradition holds that at least one inmate was shot in this part of the building while attempting to escape, and hangings were carried out in the courtyard. Are these the restless souls that are noted today in the western part of the Old Palace?

One of the best-known "ghosts" is frequently encountered in the western room called The Prince Room, for Governor Prince who, with his wife, took their residence there in the 1890s. People report seeing motion in the corners of the room and seeing faces in the fireplace. Others say that a blond woman enters the room—but never exits.

According to security guards, the same general area is the haunt of the "Clicker" for the sound it makes at all hours, but most frequently during the night and at closing time. Still more interesting are the noisier ones: the male voice that calls out to people by name, or the men who argue, yelling at each other in the old jail area. These are picked up on the guards' security devices when the building is deserted. Another one that acts up when the building is being vacated at night is the "Runner" whose footfalls can be heard on the ancient wooden flooring. An escape attempt that fails time after time? Nothing, of course, is to be seen.

The Old Palace has seen its share of life—and death. Skeletons were found buried under the floor during work on the building, showing that early residents of the structure were in the habit of using the space beneath the floor as a burial place. Wherever people live, their traces seem to last well beyond memory of who they were.

Today, the Palace of the Governors serves as a museum, the "Crown Jewel of New Mexico museums" that shows exhibits of the area's varied history. It is open Tuesday-Sunday, 10 AM-5 PM and Friday Evening 5-8 PM. Ask about special tours. It is located at: 105 W Palace Ave, Santa Fe, 87501. You may contact them at: (505) 476-5100 or go to: www.palaceofthegovernors.org to find specific staff personnel.

Photo by Daryl Black

"There's only one good reason for me to write," says Robert Jesten Upton: "to write something I'd like to read." An avid reader all his life, he's still struggling to live up to his own standard. "And I'll keep on trying," he insists.

Raised in the Southwest, it's where he's made his home—literally. He and his wife built their own house brick by adobe brick, and still love working on it. Writing is the core of his 8-to-5, as editor for the past 16 years of a weekly newsletter for librarians in New Mexico. In between, he works on his own projects. His most recent success is a first place finish in the CrossTIME Science Fiction Contest and inclusion in the *2005 CrossTIME Science Fiction Anthology*. He is currently working on a novel grown from his short story submission entitled "Cat." Robert has worked with Daryl Black, the photographer who supplied the photo included with his submission to *Ghostly Tales*, on many projects.

Ghosts Of Salem Village - 1684

Old Salem Witch Jail, Salem, MA

by Patricia Morse-McNeely

Since 1692, the ghost of an elderly man, tall and of slender build, with white hair, mustache and neatly-trimmed goatee, appears beside the Old Salem Witch Jail. He also appears regularly on Halloween, "standing mute." Who is this ghost? Why is he silent? And what would such a respectable looking fellow have to do with the jail?

Salem—the very name of this town in Massachusetts evokes the vision of witches and ghosts. It was founded in the middle 1600s by Puritans who fled from England to escape the harshness of English laws and persecutions against their religion. Yet in their own communities, they practiced the same intolerance and harshness of laws when they so much as suspected someone of being in league with the Devil.

In 1692, Salem was two towns, Salem Village and Salem Town. Salem Village was the site of the infamous witch trials, seen by some as another Inquisition as bad as what had existed in Spain during the late 1400s. Some historians compare the witch hunt to the McCarthy accusations and hearings in the 20th century. Regardless of comparisons, it is an event that affected the whole country over time and still haunts us with the ghosts of the events that occurred from February to October, 1629, when Governor Phipps, who conducted the trials of accused witches, at last abolished the Court of Oyer (to hear) and Terminer (to decide).

Today, tourists visit in hopes of seeing ghosts of witches featured in fiction and drama and to view such places as Hawthorne's House of Seven Gables (said to be haunted by one of the most prominent judges in the trials, Jonathan

Corwin), the Old Church, the Mission House, the Old Salem Witch Jail, and the cemeteries, which are said to have ghost lights at night over the graves of witches and others.

More than 150 people, male and female, were accused of practicing witchcraft, the oldest in their 80s and the youngest a four-year-old, charged along with her mother. Of that number, nineteen were hanged, the youngest a seventeen-year-old girl. One was "pressed" to death under stones, loaded on top of him slowly. It is said that most of their ghosts can be found on Gallows Hill, a steep rise near the town, where the hangings took place. Any who criticized the trials or accusations were also tried as witches. The Puritans' law in Massachusetts carried over from British law, stating that a person found guilty of witchcraft would be sentenced to death.

Where were these accused incarcerated during the witch hysteria of 1692-3? In a filthy, rat-infested dungeon that had been built in 1684. Constructed of hand hewn oak timbers and siding, the plain looking building was 70 by 280 feet. The first thing visitors might notice is the absence of bars on the windows. Odd as it might sound, the puritan ethic made prisoners accept their punishment. Anyone who did escape was generally caught and killed.

While there, the jailers stripped the prisoners to examine them for witches' marks. Both the victims and their family members were tortured to get confessions.

As if being imprisoned were not bad enough, the accused had to pay the salaries of the magistrate, sheriff, hangman, and other staff. Here are some of the "amenities" they paid for:

1. Food with a short ration of water so they would be encouraged to confess
2. The rental of fetters, chains and cuffs
3. Fees for being searched for witches' marks
4. For a bond of one pound, a prisoner could go home for the day but had to return at night.
5. If you died in jail, your family had to pay to have your

body removed.

These officials had other ways of making money as well. They sold alcohol to customers who came to play chess in the evenings, and accused prisoners with enough money sometimes bribed their way out.

In the end victims found guilty were taken from the jail by oxcart to Gallows Hill. Their dead bodies were left hanging from the branches of locust trees as an example for others to see from town.

Our story deals with Giles Corey, the one "wizard," or male witch or warlock. Corey, who was eighty years old, and his third wife, Martha, were accused by three others, who were on trial as witches. They stated that Corey's specter (invisible shape with power to torture victims) had appeared to them and forced them to write in the "Devil's Book." He and Martha were arrested on April 18, 1692, and examined by the Court of Oyer and Terminer which had been established by Governor Phipps for this purpose. For five months, the couple was jailed until Corey's trial in September.

A dozen or more people testified that he had given a sacrament of bread and wine to witches, as well as other similar testimony often attributed to witches. Corey made no reply but "stood mute" before the court. Although a full member of the Church, Corey, a prosperous farmer, was not well-liked because he was hard, obstinate, and difficult to get along with. For two days, the court asked him again and again to make a plea, but he still stood mute, knowing that to do so meant his death. He knew if he made a plea either way, he would lose his productive farm to the state. A short time before, he had deeded his farm to his two sons-in-law to circumvent efforts to take it over if he died. He also knew that by standing mute, it would mean that he would die by being pressed to death. Still he stood mute, refusing to either admit or deny the accusations.

On Monday, September 19, 1692, at noon, he was taken to

the field at the corner of Prisoner Lane, now known as St. Peter's Street, where he was stripped naked and forced to lie on the ground. A heavy board (some claim a grist wheel) was placed on his chest and heavy stones began to be piled on. Still he "stood mute." Instead of pleading for mercy or declaring his innocence or guilt, he cried out for more stones, more weight to be piled upon him so that he might die quickly. As he died, his tongue protruded from his mouth. The Sheriff stepped forward and forced it back into his mouth with his cane. Neighbors of Giles and Mary Corey witnessed this and later reported it. Giles was buried in an unmarked grave on Gallows Hill, as ordered by one of the justices, Jonathan Corwin. A few days later, on September 22, his wife, Martha, was hanged on Gallows Hill with seven others.

Giles Corey has not left Salem, however. He appears periodically beside the Old Salem Witch Jail, and always, on Halloween, he is there, a tall, slim, elderly man with a pale narrow face framed by white hair on a balding head, white moustache and neat goatee, standing mute and gazing across the town towards Gallows Hill. Though I have found nothing written or said to this effect, I wonder if his wife Martha lingers behind also. On Gallows Hill, they say, there are many ghosts of those hanged.

The town of Ipswich, which was close by and had a nice, clean jail, had housed a number of the accused witches due to the fact that Salem's jail was overcrowded. And it is said that Ipswich is also haunted by the ghosts of the Salem trials.

The following facts show the irony of the situation in 1692-93: On Oct. 29, 1692, Governor Phipps dissolved Court of Oyer (to hear) and Terminer (to decide) that he had previously established for the purpose of trying witches. On Nov. 25, he replaced it with Superior Court of Judicature, created to hear ramming cases of accused. Spectral evidence, so frequently used in witch trials to condemn, was no longer allowed. In May 1693, Governor Phipps pardoned remaining prisoners accused of witchcraft.

And what of the jail? Eventually it was closed and sold as a private residence—home sweet home! In 1863 Abner Goodell the state historian, purchased it. By 1935, the Goodell family opened the jail to the public.

Salem is located on the tip of a peninsula stretching northward, lapped on three sides by waves of the Atlantic Ocean. No major highway will carry you to Salem, but it can be reached by Highway 1A off US Highway 128. Salem Witch Jail is on St. Peter Street (the old Prisoners Lane), near the intersection of Federal Street.

Patricia Morse-McNeely, a native Texan, is the great-great granddaughter of Samuel F.B. Morse, inventor of the telegraph and American artist. She was a teacher for twenty-six years, and has been writing from early childhood. She is a prize-winning poet and a Life member of the International Society of Poets. She has memberships in the American Poets Society, the Writers League of Texas, and the San Gabriel Writers League (Texas), as well as the Society of Children's Book Writers and Illustrators. Some of her poetry can be found at www.poetry.com and a family website:

www.iment.com/maida/familytree/cousins/pat/index.htm.

A Terrible Secret - 1760
The Old Spanish Barracks, New Orleans, LA

by Patricia Morse-McNeely

In the old Spanish Barracks, in New Orleans, there lurks a terrible secret. Some question whether or not the stories told are true, but if they are, the manner in which certain soldiers were imprisoned and tortured to death is particularly disturbing and horrifying. It is an eerie, noisy, discomforting building to be in.

It may help to keep this timeline in mind: France controlled New Orleans from 1718-1762; the old Spanish (?) Barracks was supposedly built in 1760; Spain controlled New Orleans from 1762-1803; France took it back for a short time in that same year before the Louisiana Purchase gave control the United States. U.S. soldiers occupied the old Spanish Barracks by 1810 before a newer barracks was planned in 1819.

During the time of Spanish occupation, they sealed their gold in the walls of the barracks. Strongly garrisoned with troops, this gold should have been safe. But a few years after taking possession, the Spanish sent some of the soldiers to Florida on a special mission, feeling their gold was safe in the walls with only a small garrison left behind to guard it. Some of the troops left behind decided they wanted the gold and in their process to get it, decided it was best to get rid of the few who did not agree with them.

The criminal soldiers tortured and killed their compadres by hanging them on meat hooks driven into their backs and with iron spikes, nailed their feet to the wall. As a coup de grace, they tied hungry, large river rats to each one. The rats began to eat the victims alive, ignoring their screams. The thieves then sealed their victims into the wall where the gold had been—all except their faces—and watched them die. After the victims had at last died, the wall was cemented and closed fully. Then the thieves, loaded with the gold, left, never to be caught and brought to justice.

For many years those who entered the barracks were sometimes treated to the ghostly faces of the sacrificed men in the wall. Or meeting the mutilated ghostly forms of the soldiers marching back and forth in the halls of the building. Their screams and groans echoed from the building frequently. Huge, ugly rats would come through the sealed wall to startle visitors away. By a spiral staircase, witnesses also reported seeing the head of a man, perhaps the gold keeper, counting gold coins, and hearing the clink of the metal.

Because of certain time discrepancies when all of this allegedly occurred, there is considerable doubt that this event actually took place. Was there another building, another Spanish Barracks on the spot at one time? Did it really happen? Only the ghosts in residence would know—and they are not talking.

For more information see:
http://lsm.crt.state.la.us/site/cabex.htm

Author Patricia Morse-McNeely's biography can be found on page 9.

The Provost Dungeon, courtesy of Bull Dog Tours

Where Haunts Abound - 1771

The Provost Dungeon, Charleston, SC

by Eric Stabene

The Provost Dungeon is part of the Old Exchange, designed by William Rigby Naylor and constructed from 1767 to 1771. This is one of the most historic buildings in the United States. Among the many purposes it has served through the years, it was the welcome center for George Washington's visit in 1791. Many believe that if any building in Charleston is "alive," it is this one. The top floor is a reception hall. The second floor was originally used as a customs house. Today, it includes a gift shop as well as the Rebecca Motte Room, named after the founder of the Daughters of the American Revolution Chapter. In this room, two gold leaf mirrors are believed to be of European origin and have been on display since WWII.

If you look at the mirrors, you see an ordinary reflection. However, the bizarre may happen when the mirrors are photographed, producing the faint image of perhaps a cross or a bridge. Although the phenomenon is unexplained, many ghost experts believe ghosts are of an electro-magnetic state and that oftentimes film will capture the image of a ghost where human eyes cannot see it.

This is just a hint of things to be seen and felt in the lower reaches.

As a tour guide leading people into the Provost Dungeon, I would point out the architecture. It is a barrel vaulted Roman arch design, using the original bricks laid in 1771. While the Dungeon seems small, it was often packed with as many as 100 inmates at a time. The Dungeon began as a municipal jail but was used during the British occupation of Charleston to hold revolutionaries.

Further into the Dungeon, you will find what is possibly the oldest man-made structure in Charleston, part of the original walled city. In 1700 an Act of the Assembly granted permission to build the brick seawall. This section of the wall that is now exposed is known as The Half Moon Battery—"Half Moon" because of its shape and "Battery" because behind this brick half moon stood a row or battery of cannons—used to protect the city from the Spanish as well as pirates.

One of the most noted pirates was Stede Bonnet, nicknamed the "Gentleman Pirate" because he was well educated and born of a wealthy family. He even purchased his own vessel rather than stealing one as other pirates of the day did. The Gentleman Pirate was eventually captured and sentenced to hang in 1718. A large stone marker stands in Battery Park in remembrance of Stede Bonnet's hanging. Local children have a favorite saying that the ghosts of pirates "still hang out at The Battery."

In March of 2002, The Travel Channel came to Charleston to film the Charleston Ghost & Dungeon Tour for their "America's Most Haunted Places" series. Our Head Tour Guide, John LaVerne, focused on the tragedies suffered by politically assertive colonists during the Revolutionary War when the British occupied the city.

On June 28, 1776, one of the first major battles of the American Revolution took place in the Charleston harbor. The British fleet was repulsed, and Charleston remained a free and unconquered city—until May 13, 1780, when it became an occupied city. The British subsequently arrested many Charleston patriots and threw them into the Provost Dungeon, including Colonel Isaac Hayne. Others in the dungeon included two signers of the Declaration of Independence, Thomas Heyward and Edward Rutledge. The British dangled a deal in front of the patriots: sign an oath of loyalty to the King and a pledge not to take up arms against Britain, and they would be released to spend the rest of the war with their families at home. Most of the patriots refused, even though it meant the loss of their property and for some, their families.

Colonel Hayne had a particularly heavy decision. His wife and children had contracted smallpox. One child had already died, the other two were very ill, and his wife was on her deathbed. With a heavy heart and tortured soul, and at the urging of his patriot friends, Hayne signed the loyalty oath and arms pledge. He returned home to his plantation and his family. The two children recovered but his wife lingered for several weeks before dying. After her death, Hayne tried to resume his life as a planter, but the British harassed him to enlist as a British officer.

Finally, they ordered him to join the army, under threat of imprisonment if he refused. He refused, leaving his children in the care of his sister, and Hayne resumed his position as a commander of a local militia. Soon after, he was captured and thrown back into the Provost Dungeon. He was tried, convicted of treason, and condemned to be executed. The people of Charleston were outraged with the unfair treatment. However, the British wanted to make an example of a popular and public patriot and the protests fell on deaf ears.

On August 4, 1781, execution day dawned and Colonel Hayne, accompanied by a large group of friends, was marched through the streets in shackles. The British made him march past his sister's house where his children and sister stood on the porch. Overcome with grief, Hayne's youngest son cried out to his father: "Come back! Come back!"

Hayne called back: "I will if I can."

He was marched to the gallows and hanged.

Did Col. Hayne return? There are reports about the house at East Battery and Atlantic Streets where at night footsteps can be heard climbing the front porch steps on a regular basis, always walking up the stairs, a man coming home.

Some maintain that this patriot's spirit walked Charleston until the Civil War. Then they say he was so heartbroken over the Union being involved in a Civil War, he ceased to visit.

No tour guides in this company have seen Isaac's ghost or any other ghosts. However, on a regular basis, there is reason to believe that spirits could be amongst us in the Dungeon. Quite often chains around the different museum scenes will rock back and forth for no apparent reason. The brick walls are nearly three feet thick, which negates the possibility of outside vibrations.

No prisoners have been incarcerated in the Dungeon since 1782, but their spirits might be.

Editor's note: The full tour offers many more details than space allows in this chapter. Bulldog Tours offers exclusive access to these places and other sites:

Provost Dungeon – 122 East Bay St Charleston SC 29401, www.oldexchange.com

FFI: Bulldog Tours, 40 North Market St, Charleston, SC 29401, (843)722-TOUR, www.bulldogtours.com

Eric Stabene was born May 2, 1978 in Philadelphia, Pennsylvania. He did a brief stint as a tour guide for the city of Charleston before taking a corporate job in St. Petersburg, Florida. By 2002 he came back to Charleston and started working for Bulldog Tours, where he is now the manager.

In 2003 he married his college sweetheart, Susan, a graduate of the College of Charleston and the Medical University of South Carolina. Susan is an RN at Roper Hospital in Charleston, working on her master's degree in nursing. They own a house in Mt. Pleasant where they live with their two black labs, Bomer and Mason.

Photo courtesy of Louisiana State Museum, the Cabildo

Host To Ghosts - 1799

The Cabildo, New Orleans, LA

by Patricia Morse-McNeely

New Orleans is a city that dreams of the past under graceful old trees in quiet parks. It gazes on long ago lacy iron work, dignified buildings, stately mansions, somber levees looming above the Mississippi River, and ghostly nightshades mingling the present with the life that still teems from the distant past.

When I was a child of 11 or 12, I came to visit and felt right at home in the French Quarter for some odd reason—the most haunted territory, other than the graveyards, in New Orleans. I could feel the ghosts that peopled the Court of the Three Sisters, hear the shouts of sailors from the docks among the mournful voices of slaves being sold, the clatter of trolleys, shouts of street vendors, the coaxing of the ladies of the night from windows—right along with remarks of passing tourists. I sat in the park and listened to the trees recounting their stories of times past to the Gulf breezes.

If you listen with that inner ear as you explore, you may sample the wonderful flavor of the old city, still existing in the midst of modern life while you breathe its magnolia-scented breath among a ghostly crowd of perfume and ancient humanity.

Summers are hot and muggy with swamp humidity, cooled by what seems to be programmed showers that show up around two o'clock most afternoons. Lake Ponchartrain glistens like a huge pond reached by a stepped wall, hiding secrets of long ago. In the historical restaurants, on the streets, and in shops, one can hear the accents of French and Spanish, the patois of Creole and Cajun, and the soft sibilance of southern blacks mixing with American slang as a constant murmur under-ridden with the whispers of long ago.

For New Orleans is peopled by phantoms as well as living humanity. In the above-ground graveyards sometimes frequented by voodoo priests and priestesses, in the churches, all through the city, the low rumble of history makes itself known. Here wander the figures of Jean LaFitte, his brother Pierre, pirates, and their crews; James Bowie and Sam Houston of Texas fame, and many more.

The oldest jails are gone, but the Cabildo still stands proudly.

The famous Cabildo in Jackson Square, where the governments of both the French and Spanish have presided, is now the Louisiana State Museum. The town council first met in its new hall in 1799, which was the site for the Louisiana Purchase transfers in 1803 and remained the principal meeting room for the new American city council until the 1850s. The Baroness Micaëla Almonester de Pontalba was responsible for renovations to the Cabildo in the 1840s to match new construction on her own neighboring land. An entire third story was added to the building, and massive cast-iron gates were erected at the main entrance.

It once held court, and as is often the case, where court cases were tried, prisoners had to also be incarcerated. On my first visit, some 70 years ago, I remember being shown a cell—small, dark, smelling of damp, with a narrow bench on which some leg irons or heavy handcuffs lay at that time. I was told that Jean LaFitte had occupied that cell and his brother Pierre one next door after they were arrested for piracy. Jean had escaped in the night and, since he was shackled, no one knew how he managed, for the shackles lay on the floor when the cell was discovered empty. I have no idea whether this was a true ghost story or not, whether it happened or not, and cannot verify it. But there are many tales of "the gentleman pirate" LaFitte's wanderings in ghostly form in New Orleans and among the old Southern mansions.

The forerunner to the Cabildo was the French Guard House behind the corps de garde (police station). In 1769 while Spain ruled the area, a calabozo (prison) occupied the site, but it was demolished in 1837 (during American rule). Historians believe the old prison foundations were used to build two fine old, three-story antebellum houses that eventually became part of the Cabildo's offices: the Creole House at 616 Pirates Alley and the Jackson House at 619 Pirates Alley.

Also no longer standing, was the Carrollton Jail. It had originally been a fort in the early days of New Orleans to protect settlers from Indian raids and attacking pirates and rival forces of Spain and England. It became a jail sometime in the 18th or 19th century. Later it became a jail known as the Ninth Precinct of New Orleans, and that is when the stories of haunting began. The city razed it in 1937 to make way for a new building. As the courtyard tumbled down where the gallows had stood for so long, workmen claimed that amidst the rising dust, they saw figures of those who had died on those gallows grinning at them through the dusty clouds. Some said they even heard laughter.

Did the ghosts depart the area when the jail was destroyed? Could they have been inhabiting the one-time fort as far back as the 18th century?

One of the earliest accounts was told in the summer of 1899 when Sgt. William Clifton, Commandant of the Precinct welcomed two men and a young woman as visitors. In the office, the young woman leaned against the wall behind the desk. Suddenly, she was thrown to the floor by an unseen force. Alarmed, the three men could not believe what had happened. The frightened woman's explanation of her fall persuaded the men to try to disprove what she said by trying it themselves. One by one, as they leaned on the wall, they were hurled away from it with a strong force. Of course, when they related their experience to others, many disbelieved it, thinking all four people possessed wild imaginations. After all, a wall does not throw people away from it. However, all who came to the office moved or stayed away from the wall after that, and they placed a sofa against that same wall.

Several nights later, Officer Dell, a patrol wagon driver, lay down to rest on the sofa. Suddenly, the sofa moved to the middle of the room and then returned to its original position. Officer Dell's recounting of his experience naturally met raucous laughter from his fellow officers, who loudly debunked the story. They came to watch in amusement as another officer tried to lie down on the sofa. The sofa tilted and dropped the officer rudely to the floor. It is likely that others, who disbelieved or could not accept the reported incidents, came to see for themselves. Did they have similar experiences? No one else said, but everyone stayed away from the wall.

On further investigation, they learned of a man having been arrested for murdering his wife and boiling her body in lye. There against that very wall officers had beaten the prisoner to death.

In October of 1899, Officer Jules Aucoin watched a portrait of Admiral Dewey spin like a wheel on that same wall. Upon investigating, they noted that the picture was properly and firmly attached to the wall and that there was nothing on it or behind it to make it spin. As the men at the jail investigated, a mirror suddenly fell to the floor along with a framed portrait of General Beauregard in front of the witnesses. Further astonished, they investigated but could find no cause for this.

On duty one night sometime later, Corporal Hyatt heard footsteps in the hall. One foot was dragging. He got up from the desk and went to the door to see who it was. No one was there, though he still heard the footsteps. Later, it was learned that on that same night, in Pennsylvania, a lame murderer, who had escaped from this jail some time before, was found dead. Had his ghost returned to Carrollton Jail to walk the halls?

On a day in mid-July of 1899, two beautiful, smiling "quadroon girls" appeared before a sergeant on duty at his desk. To his shock, he recognized them as women who had been hanged for carving out the livers of their male companions. He was badly frightened as they stood laughing at him and then just evaporated into the air.

The most horrifying haunting of all, however, was Cell Three. Prisoners placed in the cell overnight would be found the following morning badly beaten, bloody and almost dead, and all repeated the same story: Three males would enter the cell, coming through the walls. All night they would fight the prisoner and each other. It is believed that the ghosts were those of three men who had shared the cell at one time, attacking one another so viciously that the next morning, two were found dead. The third man was so savagely mauled that a few hours after his removal from the cell, he also died.

Assignments to the Ninth Precinct from that time on were vigorously protested and numerous requests for transfer were made by those who had been there and experienced the various ghostly episodes.

In 1937, those ghosts laughed while the jail tumbled down. I wonder if they still roam the building that has replaced it, laughing at those who believe the past is dead and gone and that ghosts are only figments of our nightmares? I wonder...

The site of the Louisiana Purchase Transfer, the Cabildo was constructed in 1795-99 as the seat of the Spanish municipal government in New Orleans. The name of the governing body who met there was the "Illustrious Cabildo" or city council. Over the years, the building also served as the home of the Louisiana Supreme Court and was established as the home of the Louisiana State Museum in 1911. In 1988 the Cabildo was severely damaged by fire. Over the next five years, it was authentically restored using 600-year-old French timber framing technology. It reopened to the public in 1994 with a comprehensive exhibit focusing on Louisiana's early history. A National Historic Landmark, the Cabildo is located at: 701 Chartres St., New Orleans, LA 70116. FFI: (504) 568-6968 or 1-800-568-6968.

For more information see:
http://lsm.crt.state.la.us/site/cabex.htm

Author Patricia Morse-McNeely's biography can be found on page 9.

In the Old City Jail, photo by visitor, Gary Murray, shows unexplained lines.

Pirates, Thieves, & Civil War Soldiers - 1802

The Old City Jail, Charleston, SC

by Eric Stabene

Charleston's Old City Jail was built on a block that has been used for public purposes since the late 17th century, the first known accounts indicating that the swampy land was used as a burial ground.

Prisoners here have ranged from common thieves, murderers, prostitutes, runaway slaves, pirates, drunken sailors, and even Union soldiers during the Civil War. Conditions were nearly intolerable. What was built for 128 prisoners often exceeded 300. The jail was infested with disease, rats, roaches, and despair. It was all too common for the inmates to die long before their sentences were fulfilled. Their daily diet consisted of a nine-ounce ration of bread, a tin cup of soup (often made of spoiled meat and water), and a quart of water. A cistern in the attic gravity-fed water to cells.

Cells in the Main Cellblocks were ten and a half by eight feet, designed for one inmate per cell. In actual practice, there were as many as three. Bathrooms were chamber pots and privies. To state the obvious—due to the conditions, the prisoners had reason to turn violent towards the Jailer. In such instances, the jailer used a device called "The Crane of Pain."

The body was stretched to full length, feet fitted into a wooden box to prevent the body from swaying. Ropes were pulled taut. The prisoner was then flogged—intermittently so that the anticipation of the next lash was almost as bad as the beating itself. The jailers made sure the harsh screams were heard by all prisoners. The notorious crane's presence helped keep order.

If that was not enough, an unruly prisoner might be assigned to solitary confinement. Large rooms held as many as 40 prisoners—but not to walk around freely. Instead each prisoner had a cement coffin, shoulder width and six feet long with an open lid. You would lie on your back, and several inches above your nose and body, they sealed the coffin with an iron gate. In that casket, on your back, unable to move, and in total darkness, you spent the next several weeks of your life.

No wonder the Old Jail in Charleston was chosen to represent an insane asylum in the movie *Glory*.

A number of souls in torment may still haunt the place, but who might they be? Here's at least one likely suspect:

Innkeepers Lavinia and John Fisher may have been America's first serial killers, but early in 1820, their scheme of robbing and murdering lone travelers came to an end. Charleston authorities investigated and found the bones of almost a dozen victims beneath a bed at their Six Mile Inn. They also discovered an herb tea that would send someone into a deep sleep for hours, a beverage Lavinia served while beguiling the unsuspecting guests.

Both John and Lavinia were found guilty of murder and John was sentenced to be hanged. A city ordinance at the time prohibited a married woman from being executed. Therefore, John was hanged first, which made Lavinia a widow. Hundreds of people tried to cram into the courthouse to make sure her legendary beauty and charm would not persuade the judges to spare her life. The judges had no choice but to sentence her to death.

Outraged, Lavinia stood up in the courtroom and shouted, "If ye have a message ye want to send to Hell, give it to me—I'll carry it!"

The day of her hanging, a crowd gathered to cheer the event. She stood on the gallows, hands tied behind her back. The hangman slipped the noose over her head, and she jumped off the gallows before he had time to tighten the noose. Her neck did not snap. She dangled in the air for several minutes, strangling to death.

Lavinia was buried in the Unitarian Cemetery, the only place that would take her body, on condition that she be buried in the back without a headstone to record her existence. Today all of the old cemeteries in Charleston are well-maintained except this one. Apparently caretakers are afraid to go near it. Lavinia's ghost has been seen at the cemetery.

Ironically one of the judges who sentenced her to death is buried in the same cemetery. It is said that Lavinia's strongest presence is near her grave—and that of the judge. Her presence is also sensed in the old jail where she was housed.

The gallows that once stood outside the jail were destroyed by Hurricane Hugo. We can now only imagine the situation where prisoners inside tried to riot while the public cheered the deaths of "animals."

Picture this: wooden gallows; trap door below; noose around a neck; counter weight dropping—and the sound of the prisoner's neck snapping—contingent on the hangman's doing his job correctly.

The jail's last hanging occurred in 1906. William Marcus was tried and convicted for the brutal ice-pick slaying of his wife. 500 persons crowded into the old jail yard to watch the execution and hear Mr. Marcus say, "When I see her in Hell, I will stab her again."

During the hanging of John & Lavinia Fisher, estimates placed the number of witnesses as high as 2,000.

Surprisingly not all inmates were criminals.

In the late 1820s and possibly earlier, slave owners were allowed to keep their slaves waiting for auction in the jail yard for about 20 cents a day. Imagine 300 slaves, penned up like cattle, till the next market day...men, women, and children, crowded together in groups, or seated in circles around fires, cooking their corn or rice. Ironically, troublesome slaves were usually not imprisoned or punished in the jail. The neighboring workhouse served those purposes.

During the Civil War, Confederate forces confined Union prisoners in the jail and yard, occupied at the same time by "deserters from both armies, felons, murderers, and lewd women."

In addition to the jailer, it was normal for the town's hangman to live in the jail as well. Usually a habitual drunkard, this hangman had to be confined for several days to sober up before an execution. His payment was all he could drink. In one a case, this "professional" failed to complete his duties as expected, and the unfortunate prisoner's neck didn't snap instantly. Consequently the hangman was hanged.

The Jail was in use until 1939 and remained vacant for 61 years. Unlike most abandoned buildings, it had few problems with vandals. Why? The people of Charleston consider it to be the most haunted place in the city, and many neighborhood residents even refuse to walk on the jail side of the street. They often tell of seeing ghosts and bizarre flashes of light, as well as hearing the shrieks of the jail's lost souls.

In 1999 SOBA, School Of the Building Arts, was formed in 1999 as a non-profit organization dedicated to the preservation of the building arts in America. They purchased the jail from the City of Charleston Housing Authority for $1 with the commitment to restore it. Cost of restoration, approximately $9 million. A portion of the tours' proceeds goes to the restoration budget.

Editor's note: The full tour offers many more details than space allows in this chapter. Bulldog Tours offers exclusive access to these places and other sites:

Old City Jail (partly a college campus) – corner of Franklin and Magazine Street.

Provost Dungeon – 122 East Bay St Charleston SC 29401, www.oldexchange.com

FFI: Bulldog Tours, 40 North Market St, Charleston, SC 29401, (843)722-TOUR, www.bulldogtours.com

Author Eric Stabene's biography can be found on page 16.

Photo courtesy of the City of Augusta

Orders From A Ghost - 1811
The Bracken County Jail, Augusta, KY

by Barbara Brockwell Kelsch

I have seen "things" all my life, but didn't pay much attention to it. I thought everyone did to one degree or another. Many times I see people I don't know around other people who I know are "real." If I describe it to the person, they say "Oh, my goodness, that's so and so!" Maybe we are all around on different time layers.

Most of the time, these occurrences don't bother me, but in 2004, I experienced a puzzling encounter at the historical jail in Augusta, Kentucky where I was scheduled to conduct a tour.

The 1811 Bracken County Jail stands on what used to be the "Public Square" of Augusta. The town was part of a

Revolutionary War grant held by Captain Philip Buckner, which he donated to the county. Buckner, the county's Representative to the State Legislature, founded the city in 1797 and erected a jail, stocks, whipping posts, and pillory even before building a courthouse. The jail has its "room for debtors" and "dungeon for criminals." The latter, a log structure built from 9-inch-thick white oak logs, "let down close," had to be rebuilt after such a long time.

The jail served the city until 1967. Through the years, it has also held runaway slaves and prisoners from the riverboats. It has at times even provided classroom space for children and overnight accommodations for riverboat performers.

By 2004 the renovation of the old building was completed so that it was safe for visitors. I was one of six people who were asked to show the jail to tourists. I had done this kind of thing before in England where I had lived until 1993. My turn came on the beautiful Saturday morning of July 24th. I was to meet a troop of 20 Ohio Boy Scouts, scheduled to come across the Ohio River by ferry.

I had collected the jail key from our city office and strolled across behind the local bathing pool on my way to the jail. After I unlocked it and the lights were on, I walked around inside the left-hand wing and found all was fine. Back outside, I found the scouts had not yet arrived, so I went inside the right wing, where the iron beds and cell bars are. Suddenly I was stopped by what felt like a sheet of ice blocking my way. I thought, *Hello, we have something here.* With goose pimples on my arms, I retreated through the door into the daylight.

Immediately then I gathered my wits, turned around and went straight back in. This time I saw the figure of a tall, thin, youngish man standing there with one hand on his hip. He had a thin face and dark hair and a mustache. His shirt collar was open, and he wore dark trousers, rather dusty looking. He was outside the bars between a cell and the window.

Though I did not see him speak, the words that came out

of him were, “What are you doing here? Get out, you should not be in here!”

I turned and went back out into the sunlight.

At that point, Phil Weber, Director of Tourism, came around to inquire about the Boy Scouts who were late.

“Phil,” I said, “come inside the jail with me and tell me if you feel anything.”

He said he felt nothing. I think the poor man thought I’d lost it. He told me he would stay a while, and I could go home. That was fine with me, and back home I went.

Some weeks later, I was sitting in my studio, and my thoughts went back to that day. I sketched an impression of what I had seen. I told my husband and friends about it and showed them the drawing before putting it into my desk drawer. There it stayed all winter and the next spring.

On Thursday, May 12, 2005, our local weekly paper arrived, The Bracken County News. There on the front page was a photo of the man I had seen as a spirit the previous summer.

The article, in tribute for National Law Enforcement Memorial Month, identified the man as Augusta town Marshall Richard D. Lane, who had been shot, July 25, 1882. He was the second officer killed in the line of duty in Bracken County and the first in Augusta (according to Bracken Court Records and the Ripley Bee). The article was one of a four-part series honoring law officers killed in the line of duty in the county.

A man named Ivan W. Bowman had shot Marshall Lane in the chest with a shotgun. Although Bowman used insanity as his defense, he was convicted of murder. The 28-year-old lawman left a wife and child. His name and date of death are recorded on the National Law Enforcement Officers memorial wall located in Washington D.C. and on the state Law Enforcement wall in Richmond, Kentucky.

Until I read the article I had assumed the man I saw at the jail to be a prisoner. Only then did it dawn on me why he had not been behind bars. He would not have been in a cell, but perhaps cleaning up or guarding the place when I showed up. That would account for the young marshal's words, "What are you doing here? Get out, you should not be in here!"

As part of the renovation of the Old Jail, plans are to utilize the building as a tourist welcome center and public museum. As the oldest surviving jail on its original site in Kentucky, it was awarded the Kentucky Landmark Certificate of Registration in 1973. At this writing, the downstairs cells are restored, but the upper floor jailer's quarters, which will eventually have elevator access, are still in progress. Various groups, in addition to the City of Augusta, have assisted in saving it from further deterioration: the Bracken County Historical Society, Kentucky Heritage Council, University of Kentucky, Save Historic Augusta Restoration Effort, and Hayswood Foundation. However, additional financial assistance is always welcome.

Guided tours are available by arrangement. FFI: contact the City Offices at: 219 Main Street, PO Box 85, Augusta, KY 1002. Tourism Director, Phil Weber, (606) 756-2183 or pweber_coa@yahoo.com .

Editor's note: This is not the only spirit Barbara has identified. She once saw a woman submerged in a creek near Augusta and was so distraught about it she didn't want to return. She found in newspaper records that a woman had in fact been murdered in that fashion. Her husband's father was sheriff of Augusta in the 1950s when the woman was murdered, but Barbara, who was living in England at the time, knew nothing about the events. With the help of another psychic, they were able to set the drowned woman at peace and release her spirit to "the other side." Barbara says she finally gathered the courage to go back to the site—along with the company of her husband and two other relatives. She was relieved to see the woman's spirit is no longer suffering there.

Barbara, who misses the ghost tours so familiar in England, is currently collecting haunted stories of the area.

Barbara Brockwell Kelsch was born in England, Sept. 1, 1940. She taught art for 23 years for the Leeds and Bradford Colleges. She has also been a member of the London Guild of engravers for 15 years and has many pieces of her art work all over the world. In 1993 at the age of 52, she married an American whom she had met in 1973. Her two dogs and two cats live with her and share a beautiful garden full of flowers, trees and shrubs—all her husband's work.

The Kelsches own and operate the White Rose B&B at 210 Riverside Drive, Augusta, Kentucky 41002; phone: (606)756-2787. This old colonial home (family owned since 1917) overlooks the Ohio River and is near the ferry landing. On the premises is Barbara's art gallery where you may view her landscapes. Her husband Bob, a Latin teacher of 35 years, retired but is now back to teaching two hours a day and loves it. It was he who encouraged Barbara to talk about what she sees and to write it down.

Solid walls instead of conventional bars ensured prisoner isolation. Notice orb in upper left corner. Photo by author.

An Experiment In Solitude - 1829
Eastern State Penitentiary, Philadelphia, PA

by Dina A. Chirico

Unveiled in 1829, Eastern State Penitentiary put into effect a controversial experiment designed to modify inmate behavior through "confinement in solitude with labor." Despite being one of the most expensive buildings in the United States, an estimated 300 plus prisons worldwide are based on the Penitentiary's wagon-wheel floor plan. From the outside, Eastern State Penitentiary looks like a castle, a fortress. But when you enter and walk onto the grounds, this prison appears as an enormous, secluded array of concrete barriers.

How I came to Eastern State was quite simple. I was an active member of a prominent paranormal organization, and one of our adventures led me to this historic institution in June 2004. We arrived in the afternoon and took the last tour offered to the public. I thought it was beneficial to view the areas during daylight, so I might get some sense of the difference between day and night. We also wanted to get a sense of history.

The facility had housed some of America's most infamous criminals. Al Capone resided there for eight months in 1929-1930. In 1945 bank robber turned inmate, Willie Sutton, took credit for planning a tunnel escape with Clarence Klinedinst. Klinedinst, a prison plaster worker, also designed and helped build most of the tunnel.

How they managed to communicate is a mystery. Extreme measures were taken to keep prisoners isolated at all times. Solid walls rather than conventional bars lined the hallways so inmates couldn't see other people. Specially constructed "feed doors" and individual exercise yards minimized contact even with the guards, and when occasion required an inmate to go outside his cell, he wore a mask to prevent him from talking.

Charles Dickens, on visiting the prison, wrote, "The system is rigid, strict and hopeless solitary confinement, and I believe it, in its effects, to be cruel and wrong…"

Some people in authority may have agreed with that belief. Pennsylvania Governor Gifford Pinchot is said to have sentenced Pep, "The Cat-Murdering Dog," to a life sentence at Eastern State. Pep supposedly killed a cat that had been owned and beloved by the governor's wife. Prison records confirm that Pep was assigned an inmate number, C2559, but people disagree on the reason. According to a newspaper article, the governor sent his dog to prison to improve inmate morale.

Eastern State Penitentiary had its share of exciting events. It opened its doors on October 23, 1829, and the first escape happened in 1832 when an inmate lowered himself from the roof of the front building. Although captured, this inmate escaped again in the same manner in 1837.

1834 saw the first of several investigations into the prison's finances, punishment practices, and deviations from the Pennsylvania System of confinement. With the original prison completed in 1836, Eastern State Penitentiary cost nearly $780,000, one of the most expensive buildings of its day in the United States. In 1913, the Pennsylvania system of confinement with solitude was officially abandoned at Eastern State.

Interestingly, in July 1923, inmate Leo Callahan and five accomplices armed with pistols successfully scaled the east wall after holding up a group of unarmed guards. More than one hundred inmates escaped from Eastern State during its years of active use. Callahan is the only one never to be recaptured. All of Callahan's accomplices were apprehended, including one who made it as far as Honolulu, Hawaii.

By 9 PM on the evening of our ghost investigation, our investigative team's anticipation had increased. We met in the gift shop, signed our waivers, and heard a brief talk about where we could and could not explore. The three most desired places to search, the "most haunted cellblock," death row, and the infirmary were off limits due to the building's structurally unsound areas, but most of the cellblocks and other areas were open for investigation. The guides also mentioned two areas they could open for exploration on request, but they would need to lead us there.

My equipment consisted of a 35mm camera, a digital voice recorder, a flashlight, thermal scanner and "L" shaped dowsing rods which proved quite handy. Dowsing rods that I use, in case anyone is unfamiliar, are two "L" shaped, lightweight pieces of metal that, when held loosely, swing back and forth. This tool can pick up ghosts, electromagnetic energy, and other energy sources. When you discover an energy source, the rods will cross over each other. Most of our group captured orbs (images that look like a transparent ball of light showing up on film) which are indicative of ghostly presence, but the feelings and energy I experienced was nothing like I've felt before.

As soon as we entered, we split up into very small groups, usually not more than four. My friend and I searched together. When we entered the first cellblock, we felt like kids in a candy store. Our excitement was difficult to contain as we explored various areas of the prison. There were times we felt like there were people walking right behind us. Our hairs stood on end, our bodies cooled, and our hearts beat faster. We stated aloud that we were there to investigate and to take pictures and video, and that if they wanted to say or show us anything, we would appreciate it.

Some cells were open, and when we entered a few, nothing needed to be noted. However two open cells located toward the outside of the cellblock near the greenhouse seemed more energetic and active. The same sensations as before began again; our hairs rose, our bodies cooled, and our hearts beat faster. All this combined with the excitement of feeling you're being watched. Not only had we both experienced a strong amount of claustrophobic energy, but we came to find out that anyone who entered these two cells had generally felt the same kind of energy without suggesting this beforehand. Orbs that were photographed and the dowsing rods confirmed this.

After talking and sharing our findings with the other people on the investigation, my friend and I were alone once again. We found ourselves outside that same cellblock. By this time it was approximately 11 PM and a few people who had begun the investigation had had enough and asked one of the two guards assigned to our group to let them out.

At this point, we could hear people talking in the central rotunda, the hub where cellblocks radiated out like spokes on a wheel. They were approximately 100 feet away. We were wondering about the location of the two areas that needed a guide to open them when we heard someone walking toward us from the cellblock corridor we were outside of. Hearing only one set of footsteps, we thought by the pace of the steps it must be a guide. We turned to walk a few feet toward the opening and saw a flashlight moving around as if someone were holding it while walking through the corridor. That seemed to confirm it to be the guide.

We reached the opening, expecting someone to be in front of us. But no one was there. No flashlight, no more footsteps, no more sound. Puzzled, we peeked into the cells close to the exit in case someone had ducked in there—nothing. Surprised, but intrigued, we chalked it up to a paranormal encounter and continued our investigation with smiles on our faces.

Other investigators had captured orbs, ectoplasm, full body silhouettes on their film, and even EVP's. The latter means Electronic Voice Phenomena—the appearance of intelligible voices on recording tape that have no known physical explanation.

My friend and I left with a feeling of great accomplishment, knowing how "active" this prison is. We also developed a considerable amount of respect for the history, architecture, people, and experiences that make up Eastern State Penitentiary.

After 142 years of consecutive use, Eastern State Penitentiary closed in January 1970 and was completely abandoned in 1971. Almost destroyed by vandals, this architectural wonder soon fell into a ruin of crumbling cellblocks and broken skylights.

Eastern State is now a museum. It offers exhibits and such events as "Escape! Willie Sutton Weekend." In movies, it has portrayed a mental institution in 12 Monkeys and a Southeast Asian prison in Return to Paradise. In 2004, it received more than 100,000 visitors. The prison is located at 2124 Fairmount Avenue, Philadelphia, PA 19130. For more information: (215) 236-3300, or the website
www.easternstate.org.

Dina A. Chirico, MA, is active in the science of paranormal investigation. Some of her adventures have taken place in Gettysburg, Pennsylvania; New Orleans, Louisiana; Salem, Massachusetts; Townsend, Montana (and surrounding areas); the Lizzie Borden Bed & Breakfast in Fall River, Massachusetts; various other bed and breakfasts; and numerous cemeteries and private residences.

Her educational background includes clinical and forensic psychology, criminology, and sound therapy. She currently holds a master's degree in religion. She works as a sound therapist at Davis Centers, Inc. in Budd Lake, New Jersey (assisting mostly autistic and developmentally disabled children), and is a member of the American Society of Dowsers and the New Jersey Ghost Hunters Society, website: http://www.njghs.net.

For over 13 years, Dina has worked with energy healing modalities that include IET (Integrated Energy Therapy), Therapeutic Touch and Chakra Balancing. She resides in New Jersey with her husband, stepson, and their canine companion. She invites you to visit her personal website at:

http://home.earthlink.net/~night.orca

The Show Goes On - 1824
Weldon Theatre Built Over A Jail, St. Albans City, VT

by Tammy Petty Conrad

St. Albans City, with 12,000 residents, lies within ten minutes of the eastern edge of Lake Champlain in the Green Mountain state of Vermont, only 20 miles from the Canadian border. The smaller lakeside community of St. Albans Town is a short distance away hugging the water's edge. St. Albans, as the city is commonly known, is Franklin's county seat. Now famous statewide as the Maple Syrup Capital, it was once known as Rail City for its prominent role in the development of the railway system in Northern Vermont. The story of the northernmost battle of the Civil War highlights its extended history. Today, with its share of historical buildings, enticing boutiques and charming scenery, St. Albans provides a weekend of relaxation for overworked tourists from the bigger cities like Burlington, only 30 miles to the south. Some enjoy the natural beauty of the area.

Others experience the supernatural—whether they want to or not.

Visitors must remain vigilant for unusual, some say haunting, events. The Old Barlowe Street School has become the afterlife home of a janitor stricken by a heart attack in the 1920's. Guests are also cautioned to avoid Rublee Street where unaccounted for footsteps haunt passersby. Instead, many travel a few blocks to the family-owned Welden Theatre on North Main Street to taste the freshest buttered popcorn and catch the latest Hollywood has to offer. Often, however, they receive a repeat of what visitors have seen for years. And I don't mean reruns on the screen.

For over fifty years locals have viewed their favorite motion pictures at the Welden, named for Jesse Welden. Several other buildings and streets in town also bear his name. Although not one of the landholders in the original charter of 1763, Jesse arrived before the Revolutionary War only to be later driven off and captured by the British. Remembered as an adventurous pioneer, Welden may have been of Native American descent. Prior to his accidental drowning in 1795, corn stolen from his crib resulted in the first trial in the county with the perpetrator receiving thirty-nine lashes.

Such punishment may have looked slight compared to what used to occupy the site where this theatre was built. In 1827, fire destroyed a jail at this spot. Before knowing anything about the building's original use, new patrons often comment about an uneasy feeling. Maybe they sense the apprehension of the employees as they glance at the projection booth, wondering what will happen during the current showing. Movies have started by themselves, and unaccounted for voices reverberate in empty rooms.

Most visitors won't know that a trip to the basement usually provides a fright not to be forgotten. First, they would be surprised to find remains of the jail cells built originally in 1824, when the building confined, rather than entertained, its visitors. The first jail in the county was built in 1796. This would have been the town's fourth jail building and the second one to burn down. In 1827, a panicking prisoner almost perished before frantic rescuers created a hole in the roof of the debtor's room to extract him. Now there's a man who paid his debt to society!

The same visitors might be interrupted by an elderly gentleman in a white sweater, possibly a homeless person who took up residence years ago. He has yet to depart, although he tries, as the basement door flies open on occasion, mysteriously not setting off alarms. Could he be looking for free popcorn?

As an aside, only one execution has occurred in Franklin County. In 1820, Luther Virginia was hanged for murder, yet managed to attend his own funeral prior to his death. Maybe they wanted to make sure he was punished twice. At the courthouse, Reverend Culver aptly preached from Genesis 9:6, "Whoso sheddeth man's blood, by man shall his blood be shed." Another prisoner hanged himself during John Finn's tenure as sheriff prior to becoming Senator Finn during the late 1900s.

Digging into books at the local historical museum, tourists will discover how unusual it was to employ saint's monikers for place names in colonial New England. Puritans thought the practice smacked of papistry. Could paranormal activity in St. Albans be a direct response to this break from tradition? In 1791, St. George joined St. Albans and other communities to become part of Vermont, the fourteenth state admitted to the Union. It was the only other town Benning Wentworth, governor at the time, labeled in such a way, and some suggest Wentworth was simply trying to placate King George of England rather than memorialize a saint.

The town's name came from a hamlet in Hertfordshire, England, where a Roman soldier, later known as Saint Alban, was killed after sheltering a Christian priest. Centuries later in the same town, opposition organized against King John formed the groundwork for the creation of the Magna Carta. Historians like to believe Wentworth kept the original birthplace of civic and political liberties in mind as he named the area, but unscrupulous land trading and opposition to his Assembly's attempt to oppose the Stamp Act make this unlikely.

St. Albans' history has been as colorful as its residents. One of the oldest communities in the country, it is proud of its past and encouraged by possibilities for the future. Maybe this is why the ghosts of the Welden Theatre and other locations in town refuse to move on to the other side.

Every visitor should catch a film at the Welden as long as

it isn't a horror flick, but do avoid entering through unmarked doors. It wouldn't be smart to end up in the basement. After all, no one wants to miss the end of a movie.

The Welden Theatre is at 104 North Main Street, St. Albans, Vermont 05478.

Tammy Petty Conrad, a native Texan, spent a summer at Middlebury College in Vermont in the 1980s, but did not encounter any unusual behavior other than that of frustrated professors. In 2004, Tammy and her family returned to Central Texas after living in the United Kingdom for four years. She was only disappointed that her cottage in England, built over 150 years ago, held no surprise guests or unexpected noises. Tammy is currently completing a novel involving the Palestinian/Israeli conflict and hopes to publish a nonfiction book of her adventures in England despite the lack of paranormal activity.

Tammy is Contest Coordinator for the San Gabriel Writers' League annual writing contest (prizes in several categories). Visit her website for updates on contests and her novel: www.tammypettyconrad.com.

The American Tragedy Jail - 1834

Herkimer County Jail, Herkimer, NY

by Stacey Jones

The cell for Herkimer County Jail's most famous inmate resembles a luxury apartment more than it does the "slammer" most of us would expect.

The Herkimer County Jail, which is part of the courthouse, is located in the village of Herkimer, New York in the foothills of the Adirondack Mountains. This courthouse with jail was built in 1834 and used continuously until 1977. The majestic limestone Federal style building is situated at a four corners intersection distinguished by the National Register of Historic Places.

The jail has housed two infamous murderers. The first,

Roxalana Druse, had been sentenced to die in 1887 for the murder of her husband. With the help of her daughter, she killed him, chopped his body into pieces and buried the remains. In a sensational trial, she was tried and convicted. She was later hanged behind the jail, but according to reports, the hanging was botched, and it took an agonizing 15 minutes for her to die.

This scene so upset the officials, it prompted the New York Governor David B. Hill to examine other more "scientific" means of execution. This led to the introduction of the electric chair in 1890.

In the summer of 1906 another trial dominated the headlines across the nation. A beautiful young woman was murdered at Big Moose Lake, in the Adirondack Mountains. The Chester Gillette-Grace Brown murder case has been the focus of considerable interest. It was the basis for Theodore Dreiser's classic novel, *An American Tragedy*, and the movie A Place in the Sun.

Chester Gillette was a nephew of the owner of the Gillette Skirt Factory in Cortland, New York. He was handsome, wealthy, and considered quite the catch, not only for the women factory employees, but also rich, young society ladies. Chester met Grace at the factory shortly after she came to work. He was smitten by her beauty, and they started seeing each other. Because Grace was from a humble farming family, Chester's family felt that she was not an appropriate wife for Chester. Nevertheless, they continued to see each other. After she began to pressure him to marry, Chester broke off the relationship, but not before Grace told him she was pregnant with his child.

In the summer of 1906, Chester urged Grace to accompany him on a trip to a friend's cabin in the Adirondacks. Grace believed that Chester planned to propose and that, upon their return to Cortland, they would be husband and wife. Chester instead was planning a way out of his desperate situation. He chose the secluded Big Moose Lake area to follow through with his plan of murder.

At the lake, he rented a boat and took Grace out to a secluded part of the lake. Chester returned from the lake alone and wet, then promptly disappeared. His actions and the disappearance of Grace raised suspicion. When boaters found her body floating in the lake the next day, a manhunt ensued, and Chester was caught three days later in Inlet, New York, proclaiming his innocence.

The sensational trial took place at the Herkimer County Courthouse. Chester was housed in a special, large cell inside the jail. Separated from other inmates, he received exceptional treatment by the guards and jail administration.

During the trial, sobs of anguish were often heard throughout the halls, as Grace's family grieved while hearing the letters Grace wrote, proclaiming her love for Chester and saying farewell to her family as she anticipated a new life and family with Chester.

Gillette reportedly sat emotionless during the trial, chewing gum. The only time he spoke was when testifying that he did not kill her. He claimed that Grace fell out of the boat, and that a blow on the head she received while falling caused her death. The jury didn't believe his story, and Chester was sentenced to die in the electric chair. After his sentence, he was transferred from the Herkimer County Jail to nearby Auburn Prison. Despite many appeals and family pleas to the New York Governor, he was executed in 1908.

The ghosts of Herkimer County Jail are still spotted today. Some report seeing the ghost of Roxalana Druse wandering the halls of the jail. Often people have seen what appears to be a figure in the cell where Chester Gillette awaited his fate. And recently, the popular television show Unsolved Mysteries profiled the ghostly sightings of Grace Brown at Big Moose Lake.

Because of so many reports of paranormal occurrences, in

2001, The Historical Society called my paranormal investigation team into the jail to conduct an investigation.

The Central New York Ghost Hunters, based out of Syracuse, New York, conducted an investigation and came up with some convincing results. With various infrared video cameras, thermal scanners, cameras, and Electro Magnetic Field Detectors, they conducted a scientific investigation. During the research they witnessed a cell door handle move of its own accord. Several investigators saw a brief glimpse of what appeared to be a prison guard in a uniform, sitting at a table near a cellblock.

One investigator reportedly was shoved from behind by unseen hands, while walking down a long narrow corridor, causing her hand to be bruised. They also heard banging resounding through the halls and recorded ghostly voices on a tape recorder that said: "Hello," "Help me," and "Get Out." The jail has a life and atmosphere all its own. It demands a look at the mysterious surroundings, and you should keep in mind the troubled history that took place within its walls.

The jail is an important landmark in New York State. It still draws many visitors, and they anticipate more, when the much anticipated premiere of An American Tragedy Opera opens in the fall of 2005, at the famous Metropolitan Opera House, in New York City.

But as all old buildings do, this one is deteriorating, and there is even talk of having it razed. The Herkimer Historical Society is seeking grants for its preservation. The importance of this location, for history, education and tourism is immeasurable. Not just for its historical significance, but also for the many spirits who reside there.

Today the building houses the Herkimer County Historical Society Museum where visitors may view the many artifacts of notorious inmates housed there since 1834. You may contact the Society to ask about tours. Herkimer County Jail, 320 N. Main Street, Suite 2900, Herkimer, NY 13350.

Stacey Jones began to hunt ghosts after hearing the many ghostly stories from relatives and friends and studying the subject since 1975. In 1997 she founded Central New York Ghost Hunters, which now has over 50 members. She has been investigating claims into the paranormal since 1984. A police officer for 12 years, she holds a degree in Criminology from State University of New York, and currently resides in Cazenovia, New York. Stacey frequently lectures on the paranormal at Paranormal Conferences and colleges, including Syracuse University and State University of New York at Cortland.

CNYGH conducts paranormal investigations into residential homes, historical landmarks and dark creepy areas that ghosts haunt. The group has been profiled on numerous television stations including, NBC, ABC, CBS, and UPN. They also have appeared on radio shows including Citadel Communications, Clear Channel Radio and other radio shows across the United States. CNYGH actively raises money for many historical landmarks throughout New York State, because without these historical landmarks the ghosts would have no place to go. To contact the group, go to: www.gotghosts.org .

Man On A Rope - 1835
Rutherford County Jail, Rutherfordton, NC

by Patricia Morse-McNeely

In 1954, a group of small boys were playing near the south wall of the old Rutherford County Jail where thick, green ivy vines climbed up the brick walls.

"Pa told me there was a man on the wall behind the vine," said seven-year-old Jerry to the group.

"Aw, that's a lot of malarkey," responded another boy.

"What'd a man be doin' on a wall? How could he stand up?"

"He ain't standin' up!" remarked a third boy. "He's hangin'!"

They all laughed.

"Jerry, I dee-double dog dare ya to go look!"

Jerry strutted to the wall and pulled back the heavy vine. He stood still for a brief moment, then turned and ran toward home, his heart beating fast. The boys followed, calling after him, "What'd ja see? What'd ja see? Was a man there?"

"He's there, all right!" The frightened boy continued to run. The others took off running, too, as if demons were after them.

Today Jerry Walker Oxendine doesn't mind admitting he suffered bad dreams for weeks. But let's go back to 1880 to the events that led up to the shadow on the jailhouse wall.

Daniel Keith was a large man, standing at six-feet-four and weighing 230 pounds, all hard muscle. He had a plentiful shock of red hair and a thick red beard. Life had not been kind to him—and he returned the favor to most of the people he came in contact with.

He was born in Pulaski, Kentucky in 1848, the youngest of Clayton and Permilia Keith's eight children. When he was 13, his father died, and in 1862, Daniel left home to join the Confederate Army, which he soon deserted. Going North to Indiana, he indulged in petty thievery to survive. Later, he commented that phase of his life was a critical point where there was only one inch between going to heaven or to hell.

He found a job, but burgled his boss and returned to Kentucky where he stole a horse. Next, he went to Tennessee and re-enlisted in the CSA, only to desert again. This time he was caught, but he lied his way out of it and escaped punishment. He wandered into and through Tennessee for a number of years and finally ended up in Rutherford County, in the Blue Ridge foothills in southwestern North Carolina.

Rutherford County had been a rich land, where gold was panned daily from streams for a number of years up to 1831. Two German brothers named Bechtler opened a mint to turn the gold dust into coins. They made the first one dollar gold piece in the United States. A few Bechtler coins still exist today, possessed by people in Rutherfordton. The mint operated from 1832 to 1840 when a U.S. mint was opened in Philadelphia, Pennsylvania.

Rutherfordton was a great place for a con man like Daniel Keith. He found a truly fertile field among gullible gold seekers. His greatest swindle was a 68-pound rock that he rubbed well with brass. Using this, he sold many country businessmen a "gold mine."

His history leaves little wonder why he became one of the most hated men in North Carolina.

In January of 1880 the body of Alice Ellis, 12 years old, was discovered in the woods of Rutherford County. She had been raped and beaten to death with a large rock. Several witnesses placed Daniel Keith in the vicinity. One 16-year-old boy stated that Daniel had been drinking all day.

Shortly after the discovery of Alice's body, Sheriff Noah I.

Walker called on Daniel Keith at his cabin. When Daniel greeted him, Walker noted that the man was sober, but he had blood all over his shirt. Asked how he had gotten the stains, Daniel showed some rabbits he had been skinning. Not quite believing him, Sheriff Walker arrested him and took him to the Rutherford County Jail.

Later, he was moved to the Cleveland County Jail in Shelby as Sheriff Walker feared a lynching due to the anger spreading across the county. During the spring term of the court, Daniel Keith was tried for Alice's murder. Several witnesses testified to seeing an escaped convict from McDowell County also in the area of the murder. This man was awaiting execution for a like crime.

This evidence was ruled inadmissible due to the ruling in State vs. Baxter "...on trial of an indictment for crime, evidence tending to point to the guilt of another...does not disprove the criminality of the party charged." Therefore, despite the testimony, the jury declared Daniel guilty.

He loudly protested his innocence and swore vengeance on all who had witnessed against him or pronounced him guilty. An appeal upheld the conviction, and in September, Judge W. I. Love sentenced 32-year-old Daniel Keith to hang "until dead, dead, dead." On December 11, he remanded him to the Rutherford County Jail in Rutherfordton, just a block or two south, down the hill from the courthouse.

These were difficult days for Daniel, as well as Sheriff Walker, who had serious doubts about Daniel's guilt. Nothing in his past record of stealing and swindling had indicated any act of violence.

Sheriff Walker and others were also disturbed by the words Daniel had spoken to the Judge, jury, and witnesses before his sentencing: "The soul of an innocent man will not rest until his innocence is proved, and the Devil will take you all." Something in Daniel's voice had rung true when he said he would return to haunt them. He continued to say it morning and night as he waited.

Reluctantly, Sheriff Walker, a tall, rather stern-visaged man of 47, walked to the cell accompanied by two deputized citizens, bracing himself for the struggle he expected ahead. Daniel was almost twice as big as he was and very strong, but Daniel surprised him. Although it was obvious his anger still seethed, he stood quietly as they shackled him, tall and proud even as they seated him in a cage on a cart and chained him to the bottom of it. Beside the cage sat his coffin.

"I go blameless to the gallows," he said calmly. The cart began its slow ride up the hillside to the "hanging meadow." Sheriff Walker sat somberly, flanked on either side by his citizen deputies. Though there was a large crowd from the surrounding countryside huddling in the cold December winds from the Blue Ridge Mountains, the only sounds were the soft clop-clop of the horses' hooves and the clink-clink of the metal rings on the reins.

On the gallows platform, Daniel, tears rolling down his cheeks and sparkling in his red beard, addressed the crowd, reiterating what he had said in the courtroom and adding, "A man should be hung for what he done and not for what he ain't done." Looking at Walker, he said clearly, "Keep a cool head and don't become excited." As the black hood slipped over his head, there was a deep intake of breath by the crowd. At one o'clock, the trap door slapped open loudly, echoing across the square, and Daniel Keith dropped to his death.

Slowly the crowd, murmuring low, dispersed to their homes. A few days later, Sheriff Walker returned from his morning coffee and saw a crowd gathering at the south side of the jail.

They were all staring open-mouthed at the wall. There in gigantic relief was the shadow of a huge man hanging by the neck on a rope from the eaves of the jail. It seemed to sway slowly, and his head was canted awkwardly to one side. Daniel Keith had kept his promise. He was back.

Sheriff Walker thought it was a prank. He had the wall painted and whitewashed again and again. But the shadow returned. People crossed the street rather than walk past the south wall of the jail. Men who had come daily to have coffee with Walker no longer came.

The shadow remained, and all attempts to remove it failed. In desperation, Sheriff Walker planted ivy to cover the walls. It grew slowly to the eaves, hiding the shadow. Then came that day in 1954 when Noah Walker's descendant, Jerry, peered behind the vine to see – and the shadow was still there.

In 1949, an 85-year-old man died in a home for the aged in Rutherfordton. He had been the 16-year-old who had testified against Daniel Keith.

In 1960, the old jail was razed, leaving an empty lot. Rutherfordton citizens claim that every business built on that lot failed – a flower shop and a beauty parlor before 1975 and the Golden Skillet restaurant within a year. But today Domino's Pizza seems to be thriving.

Is the shadow gone, or is it just waiting for another wall?

Notes of interest:

Sheriff Noah Walker, a second-generation sheriff, held office from 1878 to 1884 and never carried a gun. He died in 1907.

The Courthouse, built in 1835, was located up the hill North of the Jail, between 2nd and 3rd Streets on Main Street. It burned in 1907.

Rutherford County Jail, also built in 1835, was located at the intersection of Highways NC-108 and US-221, a prime business space in Rutherfordton. It is said that strange things still happen at this spot.

The "hangin' meadow" is now the site of the Rutherfordton Hospital.

The author wishes to thank the following for their generous assistance and sharing for this story: Debra Gettys,

Adm. Asst. Chamber of Commerce; Nancy Ferguson, County Historian; Mr. Bill Byers, Pres. Rutherford Historical Society, Ms. Margaret Camby; and Ms. Betty Cochran, the latter two being direct descendents of Noah Walker. Mr. Jerry Walker Oxendine, a collateral descendent of Noah Walker, tells the story on his website:

www.ghosttoghost.com/shadowonthejail.htm.

Author Patricia Morse-McNeely's biography can be found on page 9.

Photo courtesy of Bump in the Night Tours

Secrets Of The Attic - 1845
The Old Slave House, Equality, IL

by Troy Taylor

High on a windswept rise in southern Illinois, a region better known as Little Egypt, stands a Classic Greek plantation house called Hickory Hill. Over the years, however, legends of its past as a chamber of horrors for the men and women brought here in chains, made Hickory Hill better known as the "Old Slave House." The secrets of slavery hidden here were given up many years ago, but dark whispers about the place claim that the dead of Hickory Hill do not rest in peace.

The mansion was built in Saline County by John Hart Crenshaw on the family farm, which possessed a salt well from which they started the crude salt refinery at Half Moon Lick. Today, it is hard for us to understand the importance of salt in times past. Salt was often used as barter for goods and supplies.

In the early 1800s, the westward movement created an even greater demand for salt because it could be used both for flavoring and as a preservative for meat.

The salt mines always needed workers. The labor was backbreaking, hot and brutal and attracted only the most desperate workers. Those who had escaped slavery in the South as well as free blacks from Illinois had a hard time finding anything but the lowest paying jobs. As few had homes of their own, the mine operators constructed a small village called "U.S. Salines," where the blacks could live. In 1827, that town became Equality, Illinois.

John Hart Crenshaw eventually bought several thousand acres of salt land and also owned a sawmill and three salt furnaces for processing. At one point his wealth was so great he paid one-seventh of all of the taxes collected in the state. He became known as not only a salt operator but also as a toll bridge owner, farmer, land speculator, railroad builder, state bank director, and as an important figure in both the Methodist Church and the Gallatin County Democratic party.

Despite all of these accomplishments, Crenshaw is best remembered for Hickory Hill and his ties to Illinois slavery, kidnapping, and illegal trafficking in slaves. But how is this possible in Illinois, a state where slavery was not allowed?

Illinois was technically a free state, although it did recognize three types of slavery. The slaves, and their descendants, of the French settlers along the Mississippi were protected under the Treaty of 1783. The state also allowed indentured servitude for a contracted length of time and it also allowed slaves to be leased for one-year terms in the salt lands of Gallatin, Hardin, and Saline counties. Because slavery became essential to the success of the salt operations, provision for it to continue was written into the 1818 Illinois Constitution, allowing the mine owners to lease slaves from Kentucky and Tennessee.

As imagined, the slaves had no protection under the law,

and free blacks had little more. The 1819 Illinois Slave Code gave only minimum protection to free blacks. The word of a black man could not be taken as testimony in court, and if a man was deemed "lazy" or "disobedient," he could be publicly whipped. Whites too could be fined and whipped if they provided any sort of assistance to a runaway slave, or brought slaves into Illinois for the purpose of allowing them freedom.

While the law did provide some small protection for free blacks living in Illinois, it did nothing to discourage the common practice of kidnapping them and selling them into slavery. Only civil prosecution was used to punish this practice, and few officials ever interfered with the gangs who seized blacks in river towns and carried them down south for sale at auction.

"Night riders" of the 1830s and 1840s, on the lookout for escaped slaves, posted guards along the Ohio River. Slaves they captured were ransomed back to their masters or returned for a reward. They also kidnapped free men and their children, and sold them in the south. The nightriders created a reverse underground railroad.

Tradition has it that John Hart Crenshaw, who leased slaves to work the salt mines, kept a number of nightriders in his employ, a profitable sideline to his legitimate businesses. By law, Crenshaw's men could capture the runaway slaves and turn them in to a local law officer for a reward. If no reward had been offered for the runaway, the county paid a flat $10 fee. Crenshaw could then lease the slave from the county at a lower rate. However, many believe that Crenshaw had little interest in rewards and leases. He learned that he could make much more money by simply working the captured slaves himself or by selling them directly back into the southern market. While there exists no written evidence that Crenshaw was involved in illegally holding slaves, it has long been believed that he was.

The public had no suspicion that this pillar of the church

and community would do such things. They would have been even more surprised to learn that the slaves were being held captive in the barred chambers of the third floor attic of his house.

Here, men were often subjected to cruelty and women to the "breeding chamber." It was in this chamber, the stories say, the women and girls met a slave called "Uncle Bob." A giant of a man, he had been chosen as a stud slave because of his intelligence and physical size. Better and stronger slaves could earn more money for Crenshaw at auction. A pregnant slave on the southern market was worth nearly twice as much as a female with no child. Crenshaw was believed to have sold excess slaves he didn't need on his farms and in the salt mines. The practice turned a handsome profit and kept him supplied with workers.

According to "Uncle Bob," or Robert Wilson as he came to be called, he sired no fewer than 300 children in a span of ten years at Hickory Hill. Historians have more than forty affidavits from people who met and talked with Wilson about his life in service to Crenshaw. After leaving southern Illinois, Wilson served in the Confederate Army during the Civil War. He lived to be 112 years old and died in the Elgin Veteran's Hospital in 1949.

Hickory Hill, built in the Classic Greek style of the time period, rises three stories and was completed in 1842. It stands on a high hill, overlooking the Saline River. Huge columns, cut from the hearts of individual pine trees, span the front of the house and support wide verandahs. On the porch is a main entrance door and above it, on the upper verandah, is another door that opens onto the balcony. Here, Crenshaw could look out over his vast holdings. He furnished the interior of the house with original artwork and designs that had been imported from Europe. Each of the rooms, and there were thirteen on the first and second floors, were heated with separate fireplaces.

The house was certainly grand, but the most unusual

additions to the place were not easily seen. Legend has it that there was once a tunnel that connected the basement to the Saline River, where slaves could be loaded and unloaded at night. In addition, another passageway, large enough to contain a wagon, was built into the rear of the house. According to the stories, this allowed slaves to be unloaded unseen from the outside. The back of the house is still marked by this carriage entrance today.

Located on the third floor of Hickory Hill are the infamous confines of the attic, proof that Crenshaw had something unusual in mind when he contracted the house to be built. The attic is reachable by a flight of narrow, well-worn stairs. They exit into a hallway, 12 feet wide and 50 feet long, faced by about a dozen cell-like rooms with barred windows and flat, wooden bunks. Originally, the cells were even smaller, and there were more of them, but some were removed in the past. One can only imagine how small and cramped they must have been because even an average-sized visitor to the attic can scarcely turn around in the ones that remain.

The only cell that is bigger than the rest is the one designated as "Uncle Bob's Room," but even this chamber only measures nine by twelve feet. The corridor between the cells extends from one end of the room to the other. Windows at the ends provided the only source of light and ventilation, and during the summer months, the heat in the attic was unbearable.

Slaves were chained to heavy metal rings in their cells that left scars on the wooden walls and floors. Chains and heavy balls are still kept on display, as are two frames said to have been whipping post stands where slaves were flogged for disobeying orders or failing to complete their work. According to written accounts, the whipping posts were "built of heavy timber pegged together. A man of average height could be strung up by his wrists, and his toes would barely touch the lower cross-piece."

Stories have long been told about the cruelties that Crenshaw inflicted on the slaves, from beatings to disfigurement. Owners of the house have told many, but even worse are the stories passed on by descendants of the Crenshaw family. One relative recalled stories told by her grandmother about the family being forced to watch when the slaves were whipped. Other descendants swear that Crenshaw was unjustly accused of such crimes.

Ironically, in September 1840, Hickory Hill played host to a guest who would someday achieve fame not only as an American President, but also as the man who emancipated the slaves. According to tradition, when Abraham Lincoln was in Gallatin County for a series of debates held in Equality and Shawneetown, he attended a party at Hickory Hill in honor of the politicians. Following the customs of the time, Lincoln then spent the night at the house along with several other guests. Whether or not he ever learned the secrets of the house's attic is unknown.

In 1842, Crenshaw was indicted on criminal charges. According to the Illinois Republican newspaper in Shawneetown, Crenshaw ordered his men to abduct a free black woman named Maria Adams with her children from their home. They were kept hidden for several days, then tied up in a wagon and driven out of state. Unfortunately, the prosecutor in the court case knew more than he could prove, and Crenshaw was again set free.

Soon, rumors began to spread about Crenshaw's business activities. Around the same time, a newspaper account publicly declared that a nephew of Crenshaw was accusing him of cheating him out of his father's estate. These rumors and rumblings, combined with the Adams indictment, started to upset a lot of people in the area. On March 25, 1842, a steam mill that Crenshaw owned in Cypressville was burned to the ground just two days before Crenshaw's trial began in the Adams case and although no one was killed in the blaze, two of the workers were injured and badly burned. The fire was believed to have been started by a group of free black men, angry over Crenshaw's actions.

By 1846, Crenshaw's business holdings in general began to decline. To make matters worse, Crenshaw was also attacked by one of his slaves, resulting in the loss of one leg. The stories maintain that he was beating a woman in his fields one day when an angry slave picked up an ax and severed Crenshaw's leg with it. After that, most of the slaves were sold off, and his operations dwindled with the end of the salt mining.

During the Civil War, Crenshaw sold Hickory Hill and moved to a new farmhouse closer to Equality. He continued farming but also diversified into lumber, railroads, and banks. He died on December 4, 1871 and was buried in Hickory Hill Cemetery, a lonely piece of ground just northeast of his former home.

Whether John Crenshaw rests in peace is unknown, but according to the tales of Little Egypt, many of his former captives most certainly do not. According to the accounts, "mysterious voices can be heard in that attic, sometimes moaning, sometimes singing the spirituals that comfort heavy hearts."

And those accounts, as the reader will soon learn, are just the beginning.

I have visited the Old Slave House more than a dozen times. The attic of the house is still quite disturbing. There has never been a time when I have climbed that old staircase to the third floor that I have not felt my heart clench a little. The remains of the slave quarters are often hot and cramped, and at other times, are filled with mysterious chills that no one seems quite able to explain. I have yet to encounter one of the ghosts of Hickory Hill, but others have not been so lucky. Could the tormented souls of the slaves still linger in the attic?

I have spoken with George Sisk, the last private owner of

the house, on many occasions. "The house is haunted," he insisted. "I don't believe in ghosts but I respect them." This curious statement of non-belief was followed by the assertion that he never went into the attic of the place unless he had to. On those occasions, he never stayed long, and if no one else was in the house, the door to the attic was always kept locked.

Is the house haunted? Based on the stories, most likely it is, but the Sisk family did not create the ghost stories of Hickory Hill. That distinction belongs to the scores of visitors who have come to the house over the years and who have encountered something beyond the ordinary. The house had been in the Sisk family since 1906, when George's grandfather purchased it from a descendant of John Hart Crenshaw. It was already a notorious place in the local area, but it would soon become even more widely known.

To locals, the house was known more as the "Old Slave House" than as Hickory Hill, thanks to the stories surrounding the place. In the 1920s, visitors from outside the area would come to the Sisk's door at just about any hour and request a tour of the place, having heard about it from a local waitress or gas station attendant as they were passing through.

Thanks to a savvy advertising campaign, the Old Slave House, became a destination point. Tourists were so numerous that in 1930, the owners began charging admission. For just a dime, or a nickel if you were a child, you could tour the place where "Slavery Existed in Illinois," as the road signs put it. Soon Hickory Hill was one of the most frequently visited places in Little Egypt. And soon, it would gain a reputation for being the most haunted one.

Tourists began reporting strange happenings. They heard odd noises in the attic especially, noises that sounded like cries, whimpers, and even the rattling of chains. A number of people told of uncomfortable feelings in the slave quarters, sensations of intense fear, sadness, and of being watched. Cold chills filled a number of the tales, along with being touched by invisible hands and feeling unseen figures brush by them.

The rumored hauntings brought even more people to the house. Other legends soon began to attach themselves to Hickory Hill. The most famous is the story that "no one could spend the entire night in the attic." The story got started because of an incident involving a "ghost chaser" from Benton, Illinois named Hickman Whittington. The Benton newspaper, the Post-Dispatch, noted in a late 1920s edition that "whether ghost chaser Hickman Whittington expects to see a white or black ghost remains to be seen. He said he recently learned that cries have been heard coming from the post where slaves were whipped for disobedience, and he intended to do something about it."

But whatever happened to Whittington after coming to the house that night scared the life right out of him. I was told by one of his descendants that, according to family lore, he was in fine health when he left the Old Slave House, but just after arriving home, he sat down to have dinner and simply fell over dead into his plate of mashed potatoes.

George Sisk had no response for what that "something" could have been. "I wouldn't want to be the one to say," he said, "but it could have been the same thing that scared those two Marines that tried to stay in the attic overnight in 1966. They had the good sense to leave before anything disastrous happened…they came flying down the stairs at about one-thirty in the morning. Said they saw forms coming at them. They were in a state of shock. I really didn't get to talk to them very long. They tore out of here in a hurry...didn't even bother to go back upstairs to get their belongings."

What had they seen? The two Marines, who had both seen action in Vietnam, were certainly not the first to give up. After the incident involving Hickman Whittington and the story that no one could make it through the night, literally dozens had tried. None of them had been successful, but the two veterans were sure they would be the first. Each of them scoffed when they were told that others had fled the house in terror. After several hours in the attic, the Marines began to get bored. Finally, just as they were about to go to sleep, their kerosene lantern began to flicker. There were no drafts but the light began to get dimmer and dimmer. Then, an agonized moan filled the air, seeming to come from all around them. The moaning was followed by other voices and then, just before the lantern blew itself out, the Marines claimed to see "swirling forms" coming out of the shadows. Terrified, they fled the attic and never returned.

Other would-be thrill seekers followed, but for one reason or another, no one managed to make it until daybreak in the attic of Hickory Hill. One night a small fire got started by an overturned lantern. After that Mr. Sisk turned down requests for late night ghost hunting.

He only relented on one other occasion. In 1978, he allowed a reporter from Harrisburg named David Rodgers to spend the night in the attic as a Halloween stunt for a local television station. The reporter managed to beat out nearly 150 previous challengers and became the first person to spend the night in the slave quarters in more than a century. Sisk told newspapers, "Other reporters before Rodgers had tried to stay the night, but none of them made it. They all said they heard shuffling feet and whimpering cries in the slave quarters at night."

Rodgers later admitted that he was "queasy" going into the house and also said that his experience in the attic was anything but mundane. "I heard a lot of strange noises," he said the next morning. "I was actually shaking. The place is so spooky. The tape recorder was picking up sounds that I wasn't hearing." He felt pretty good about himself afterward, but confessed that he "didn't want to make the venture an annual event."

Stories from visitors and curiosity seekers have continued over the years. George Sisk even witnessed one incident. A woman came down from the attic one day and asked about the peculiar things going on up there. He and his wife followed the woman back to the attic and she showed them how, in certain locations, all of the hair on her arms would stand on end. She demanded to know why it was happening, but of course no one could tell her.

I have since spoken with others who have had similar experiences and with other witnesses who claim to have been touched and poked by fingers and who have heard the now famous voices and mumbling snatches of song that have long been reported on the third floor.

For most visitors though, a visit to Hickory Hill is not so bizarre. Many experience nothing, while others say they feel unsettled or frightened in the attic. Often, emotions become overwrought here and grown men have been reduced to tears. Proof of the supernatural? Perhaps not, but the attic is certainly an odd place with a haunted past.

In 1996, the Old Slave House was closed down, due to the declining health of Mr. and Mrs. Sisk. Although it looked as though the house might never re-open, it was finally purchased by the state of Illinois just over three years later. Plans are in the works (as of this writing) to open the house again in the future as a state historic site. What will become of the ghosts, or at least the ghost stories, is unknown. As many readers know, legends and lore don't often fare well at official state locations.

Regardless, if you should get the chance, mark Hickory Hill as a historical and haunted place to visit. If you climb those stairs to the attic, you will feel your stomach drop just a little, and you might even be overwhelmed by sadness.

Is it your imagination, or does the tragedy of the house still make itself felt? I can't say for sure, but I can guarantee that you will find yourself speaking softly in the gloomy, third floor corridor as your voice lowers in deference to the nameless people who once suffered here.

Hickory Hill plantation house still stands today, although some would like to see it torn down. It is located near the town of Equality, a short distance from Harrisburg. The border of Kentucky, where Crenshaw stationed his "slave catchers" on the river at night, is just a short horseback ride away.

For further information, visit
www.dailyegyptian.com/fall98/10-28-98/slaves.html
or the author's website:
www.prairieghosts.com.

Editors note: For further developments on the fate of the house, go to: www.illinoishistory.com/oshpage.html. On July 14, 2004, the Old Slave House was nominated for the National Park Service's Underground Railroad Network to Freedom program. According to the site, "Despite's the site's status as a station on the Reverse UGRR, the legislation creating the program also authorized the NPS to recognize such kidnapping sites as well." Two more recent notations from the same website mentioned an online newsletter from "Open it NOW! Friends of the Old Slave House" and this update: "Aug 17, 2004 – The National Park Service is now taking comments on the application of the Old Slave House to join their Underground Railroad Network to Freedom program," with directions for how to do so. Watch for how this goes.

Troy Taylor is the author of nearly 40 books about history, hauntings, and the unexplained in America, including Haunted Illinois, Haunted Chicago, and Weird Illinois. He is also the founder of the American Ghost Society, a network of ghost hunters from all over the country. On a variety of paranormal subjects, Taylor has spoken to literally hundreds of private and public groups, appeared in newspaper and magazine articles, has been interviewed hundreds of times for radio and television broadcasts, and has participated in a number of documentary films, television series, and one feature film.

Born and raised in Illinois, Taylor has long had an affinity for "things that go bump in the night" and published his first book in 1995. For seven years, he was also the host of the popular, and award-winning, "Haunted Decatur" ghost tours of the city for which he sometimes still appears as a guest host. He also hosted tours in St. Louis and St. Charles, Missouri, as well as in Alton and Chicago, Illinois. He and writing partner, Ursula Bielski, are co-owners of the Bump in the Night Tour Co., www.prairieghosts.com which hosts overnight excursions to haunted places throughout the Midwest.

He currently resides in Central Illinois in a decidedly non-haunted house.

The Huntsville Walls - 1849

Huntsville State Prison, Huntsville, TX

by Mitchel Whitington

The notorious "Walls" Unit of the Huntsville State Penitentiary has certainly seen its share of misery. Not only has it housed some of the country's most heinous criminals, it is also the place where inmates with a death sentence are executed in the State of Texas. Between 1849 and 1923, the method of execution was by hanging. The state then approved the electric chair as the preferred method, and "Old Sparky" was born; it was constructed by inmates, and used to terminate 361 human lives. Capital punishment was declared "cruel and unusual" by the U.S. Supreme Court in 1972, and executions were halted at the Walls Unit. The death penalty was re-instituted in 1976, and lethal injection was introduced as the method for carrying out the sentence. As of 2005, 355 prisoners were executed in the Walls Unit by the needle and three drugs given in a deadly sequence: Sodium Thiopental to induce a coma in the condemned prisoner; Pancuronium Bromide, a muscle-relaxant to cause the collapse of the diaphragm and lungs; and finally, Potassium Chloride to stop the heart. The whole process takes under ten minutes.

In the past ten years, one third of all the executions in the United States have been carried out in the Walls Unit of Huntsville. With all the death within those walls, it should be no surprise that supernatural stories began to surface about the place over the years.

The history of Huntsville State Penitentiary goes back to 1848, when the Texas legislature saw a need for organized incarceration and passed a bill to establish a state prison. The governor appointed three committee members: John Brown of Henderson County, William Palmer of Walker County, and William Menefee of Fayette County. Together they selected Huntsville as the home for the new prison facility; their reasoning in selecting that city is a mystery to this day. Perhaps the fact that there was a local rally to attract the prison played a major part, or even that the town was the home to Sam Houston; no matter what the reason, Huntsville was chosen.

Construction began late in 1848, and in a year's time the workers had finished most of the ground floor of the first brick cellblock, and expected to complete the entire structure later in the year. In anticipation of possible construction delays, prison officials had erected a makeshift jail of heavy logs and iron bars to house any prisoners who might arrive before the permanent structures were completed. In these temporary cells the first prisoners were confined when they arrived on October 1, 1849.

The prison was soon completed, and the Walls Unit – one of the first buildings constructed at the prison, and named after the 32-foot-high brick wall that surrounds the facility – was slated to become the death house. Over time strange, ghostly happenings began to be reported there. An inmate named Sam Houston, who was named for the legendary hero of Texas, was in and out Huntsville State Prison for different crimes and apparently encountered several apparitions during his tenures there. On one instance, for example, a guard was escorting Houston between the east and south wings, where a heavy armored door separated the two sections. Houston is said to have seen a spectral form in prisoner's garb step right through the door. As the story goes, he turned to the guard and asked if he'd seen the sprit. The guard said, "I sure did."

Another spirit said to frequent the Walls unit is the "Ax Man," a ghost who strolls down the hallway carrying a head in his hands. Sam Houston swears to have seen him, as have other inmates through the years.

The ghost of Chief Satanta of the Kiowa Indian tribe lingers in an area between the Walls unit and the walkway to the Death Chamber. On October 11, 1878, while the Chief was serving out a life sentence at the prison, he complained to the prison physician about a pain in his chest. He was taken to the prison hospital on the second floor, and when the doctor left him alone for a moment, the eerie strains of the Kiowa death song were heard issuing from the room. Satanta leapt headfirst from the second-story balcony to the ground below, killing himself rather than remaining imprisoned. Today a flowerbed marks the place where he died, and his presence has been reported there throughout the years by prisoners and corrections officers alike.

The haunting of the Walls Unit isn't restricted to specific ghosts, though. Guards have heard the clanging noises of cell doors opening and closing, when it would literally be impossible for that to occur.

Directly below the South Wing is the old "Death Row" of the prison, containing nine small cells where prisoners spent their last days on Earth. The area is no longer used – the cell doors are open, and the death chamber where many inmates fell prey to the terrible electric chair has been sealed. The Death Row section is basically underground, and visitors there report a feeling of doom and dread. This area of the prison seems to be especially haunted, and probably with good reason. In an October 29, 1999 story in The Austin American-Statesman, the reporter told the story of a Prison Supervisor who placed a voice-activated tape recorder in the old death row section: "When he played it back later for several correctional officers, they heard the clanging of cell doors and at the very end an unidentified voice saying 'Hey captain, hey captain…'"

There will probably always be a need for the Huntsville State Penitentiary, and the ghost stories from the Walls unit will probably continue to be told as well.

Huntsville State Penitentiary is located in Huntsville, Texas, and is an operating prison facility… which means that if you'd like to investigate it, there's only one sure way to get inside.

Mitchel Whitington is an author and lecturer on the paranormal. He has explored haunted locations from coast to coast, incorporating his experiences into his writing and speaking. Originally born in East Texas, Mitchel returned to the Pineywoods section of Texas several years ago. He has an 1861 home in Jefferson, Texas named The Grove, which he shares with his wife, basset hounds, and several spirits.

Fort Warren, photo by Paul F. King

The Bridgewater Triangle - 1854

Taunton Lunatic Asylum/Jail, Bristol County, MA

by Janet L. Kilgore

"Lizzie Borden took an axe
And gave her mother forty whacks,
And when she saw what she had done,
She gave her father forty-one."

American children jump rope to this gruesome verse, the horror of the event not registering in their young minds. The ditty stays with you for life and influences your concept of life in New England. The Salem witch trials and the Lizzie Borden murders get a lot of attention when people write about haunted places in Massachusetts, but many lesser-known souls still roam the sites of their tortured lives. The very nature of jails makes them magnets for these restless spirits and other unexplained phenomena.

Not all the state's jails are haunted, however. As a matter of fact, that most famous of axe murderers, Lizzie Borden, is not known to haunt the scene of her crimes, the jails in which she was held until her acquittal, nor the house she bought after the trial. On August 15, 1892, the Taunton Daily Gazette reported, "...Lizzie did nicely at Taunton [jail], was treated well, and when it was thought to transfer her to New Bedford for the duration, she asked and was given permission to remain at Taunton until the trial. She and her sister, Emma, visited later, after her trial."

Frequently, layer upon layer of pain, sadness, and violence build up over the centuries, until an area seems to be a portal for those "on the other side" and general paranormal activity. A 200 square mile area in Massachusetts, known as the Bridgewater Triangle, is such a place. The triangle, formed by drawing lines from Abington to Freetown to Rehoboth, includes seven of the towns in Bristol (the Cursed) County.

Not only does this area report a great deal of traffic back and forth between our world and the other side, but it also seems to act as a magnet for evil doings. A disproportionate amount of violence and suicide is reported in this area. Religions and sects based on nature worship, such as Wiccans, abound here, but darker cults are drawn to the area as well. Rumors of satanic cults and their bloody rituals in the Triangle have circulated for 400 years.

Some of the most psychically active jails in the Bridgewater Triangle started out as mental hospitals. Nineteenth century treatments for mental patients—called the Moral Treatment—were to isolate, secure against escape, and try out the latest cure on the hapless residents. When mental health treatment became more medicine-based in the 1950s, many of these foreboding gothic buildings were abandoned and left to rot.

Although many of the original buildings are now closed and in disrepair, the old Taunton Lunatic Asylum is one of the twelve mental hospitals built to the specifications of Dr. Thomas Kirkbride, a pioneer in more humane treatment of the mentally ill. It is currently in use by Massachusetts Department of Youth Services, the Department of Mental Health, and the Department of Social Services.

Contributing writer for www.masscrossroads.com, Christopher Balzano, says, "It houses convicted juvenile offenders and offers care to wards of the state and the youth of Massachusetts with specific and nonspecific mental health issues, many of whom have a history of violent behavior. [Modern residents] create a layering in the energy of these buildings. If you believe in ghosts, these are perfect places for them to flourish. Decades of pain, death, and experimental treatment mix with modern pain, death, and experimental medicine.

"[The facility] now goes by the nickname Taunton Secure and has created fear among its residents and staff. Given the nature of the clientele, the history of the building, and the highly emotional energy of the building, it is not surprising you can find several different spirits calling the jail home," Balzano says.

During Taunton Secure's days as a mental asylum, rumors abounded of cult activity at the hospital. There are stories of staff members bringing the more incapacitated patients to the basement for bizarre satanic rituals. There are even rumors of patients being sacrificed, and occasionally, the appearance of Satan himself. Strange symbols that remain on the basement walls provide more questions than answers.

As intriguing as the stories of sightings of souls from long ago are, perhaps the most reliable stories come from more modern times, related by people familiar with today's science.

Credibility is lent to the stories by the numerous experiences of current residents and staff members in the basement. Some report cold spots that seem to move with them. One staff member says he stopped on the bottom step because a strong sensation hit him. He felt he was experiencing the terrible things that had occurred there. He quit the next day. Many residents, most of them toughened by their criminal pasts, simply refuse to go into the basement to do chores, even though it means their sentences will be lengthened for non-compliance.

The strange happenings are not confined to the basement. Residents have had their lights turn on and off in the middle of the night, and many have seen a shadowy man. He appears to residents after a particularly bad day, as if he feeds off their negative emotions. One resident escaped from the building and hid out in one of the many cemeteries around the facility. As he crouched by a tombstone, he heard indistinct whisperings but saw no one. Then the whispering stopped, cold hands grasped his shoulders, and he clearly heard the word, “Leave!” He quickly walked back into the facility and gave himself up.

A more modern lockup for youthful offenders in the Bridgewater Triangle, the Crystal Springs School, near Rehoboth, also has ghosts. Several staff members report hearing the voices of former residents in areas off limits to current residents. Many report hearing the sounds of small children, who are never in the building. An old woman and a young boy have been seen walking the halls, and a ball of white light that disappears through doorways has been reported.

The most disturbing apparition is of a young man in his mid-twenties who wears a leather bomber jacket and appears out of nowhere. He has been seen inside the facility and under a streetlamp outside, but he disappears into nothing. He never attended the facility, but a man resembling his description was killed on the road just outside the property a few years ago.

Some places in Massachusetts leave you wondering if ghosts outnumber the living. Such a place is Boston, north of the Bridgewater Triangle. It is home to one of the state's most famous ghostly legends.

Ft. Warren, located on George's Island in Boston Harbor, was a Union prison during the Civil War. Shortly after Lt. Andrew Lanier and 600 other Confederate soldiers were imprisoned there, Lanier's wife began planning their escape. Dressed as a man, she managed to break into the prison and find her husband. She smuggled in a shovel, a pickax, and a pistol. The prisoners began a tunnel to the armory, but it was discovered just as they reached their goal. The soldiers surrendered, but Mrs. Lanier drew her pistol and fired at a Colonel. The damp gun misfired, and the fragmented bullet struck and killed her husband.

When Mrs. Lanier was sentenced to hang, she requested only that she be allowed to wear a dress. A black dress was found, and she met her fate on the gallows. Seven weeks later, the Lady in Black began haunting the fort. A night sentry felt two hands around his neck and turned to see Mrs. Lanier trying to choke him to death. Her ghostly footprints have been found in the snow, and she has appeared to many soldiers over the years. A sentry during World War II was so frightened by the Lady in Black, he spent over twenty years in a mental institution.

While visiting Massachusetts, consider a paranormal trek from the Lizzie Borden Museum, (230 2nd Street, Fall River, MA, 508-675-7333,) through the Bridgewater Triangle, including Taunton Secure (60 Hodges Ave., Taunton, MA 02780-3034, 508-977-3000) and Crystal Springs School near Rehoboth, (38 Narrows Rd., Assonet, MA, 508-644-3101), to Boston's St. George Island (for information contact the Metropolitan District Commission, 20 Somerset Street, Boston, MA 02108, 617-727-5215), to the Salem Witch Museum (Washington Square North, Salem, MA 01970, 978-744-1692).

Photo by Mark Ashley

Janet L. Kilgore is a freelance writer based in Austin, Texas. She has been writing professionally for over ten years in genres including history for children, magazine and newspaper articles, ghost-writing (no pun intended), and writing about ghosts in Joan Upton Hall's book, *Ghostly Tales from America's Jails*. Her on-going projects include collaborating with Joan Hall on a monthly humor column ("Hall & Kilgore") and a monthly column on tent camping ("The Happy Camper") for *The Williamson County Sun*, and ghost-writing a self-help book (working title *Power Structure*).

Kilgore also works at a local high school, substituting frequently and giving presentations on historical period fashions. She is a member of the San Gabriel Writers' League and has given presentations on writing humor and writing for magazines.

Currently working on a series of short stories about members of her family, Janet plans to publish them with original, down-home recipes from each person—and healthier, light versions she has developed. Mrs. Kilgore and her husband have two children, three grandchildren, and a dog that looks like Yasser Arafat. Her favorite saying is, "Be grateful if you have crazy people in your family; it gives you something to write about."

Doin` Time On The Rock - ca. 1850s
Alcatraz Prison, San Francisco, CA

By Mitchel Whitington

Okay, so it wasn't actually all that much time. A few hours at the most – but I spent a wonderful, cool, June morning exploring the iconic old prison called Alcatraz.

"The Rock" – no other prison in the world is known by so simple a moniker. It is a name, however, that accurately reflects the desolation and despair of the place.

Situated in the middle of San Francisco Bay, it has a mysterious past, legends of which began long before European settlers came to North America. According to some oral histories, the Ohlone Indians who lived in the area were the first to use the island for a prison, of sorts. Those who violated tribal law were banished to live there, isolated from the rest of the tribe.

In 1775, Spanish explorer Juan Manuel de Ayala saw the island and named it "Isla de los Alcatraces", or Isle of the Pelicans, because of the large population of Pelicans that he found nesting there. That name was eventually shortened to Alcatraces, and then "Anglicized" to Alcatraz.

The island was pretty much ignored for the next several decades, until the California gold rush brought settlers streaming into the area. The United States government soon took note of the burgeoning growth of San Francisco, and realized the need to have a defensive position in the bay. A Presidential Order signed in 1850 by Millard Fillmore designated the island as a military installation, and in only a few years a military fortress had been built on top of the island. By 1854 the lighthouse had been erected, and provided a beacon to shine across San Francisco Bay.

It soon became apparent that the heavily armed fortress was an excessive reaction of the Federal Government – there had never been a hostile incident, and the huge cannons had never been fired. Because of its seclusion, another use for the island was evident, and the military began to house its prisoners there in the late 1850's. This would continue for the next eighty years.

In 1909 the fortress was torn down so that a full-fledged military prison could be built; only the basement cells were left. Inmates provided the labor, and in 1911 the new facility opened. It was officially named, "U.S. Disciplinary Barracks for the U.S. Army, Pacific Branch," but the prisoners gave it a new nickname: The Rock. It was under military control until 1933, when Alcatraz was signed over to the United States Department of Justice.

During the 1920s and 30s organized crime was running rampant in America, and the government needed a way to demonstrate that there would be no tolerance of the most heinous offenders. The cold, foreboding image of The Rock provided just that. Until its closing in 1963, the prison was the lockup for criminals that were almost household names: Robert "The Birdman" Stroud, George "Machine Gun" Kelly, mobster boss Al Capone, bank robber Leon "Whitey" Thompson, and Alvin "Creepy" Karpis. The roughest, toughest, meanest villains walked the concrete hallways of Alcatraz.

The final decision to close the prison facility came strictly because of the excessive cost of operation. It was the most expensive installation in the justice system, a fact that could no longer be ignored. On March 21, 1963, the cell doors were locked – in that capacity – for the last time.

The island unofficially opened again in November of 1969, when a group of Indians led by Richard Oakes set out to claim it for their people. They presented a list of demands to the American government, and vowed to occupy Alcatraz until they received what they wanted. The officials basically ignored the situation, letting it play out on its own, until June of 1971 when a small band of Federal Marshals removed the remaining people from the island.

The island was designated as a National Park in the early 1970s, and in 1973 the first tourists were taken there by boat. It wasn't long, however, until the visitors and staff began to report strange happenings.

The mumbling of male voices was heard emanating from cells that were closed and empty. Footsteps echoed down the concrete floor of Broadway and other legendary passages between the cellblocks. An occasional sobbing has echoed down the hallways, and unpleasant odors form clouds that move through the corridors. Phantom prisoners have been seen, as have civil war soldiers.

Armed with all those ghost stories – but no specific locations, since I'd purposefully stayed away from any details before the trip – I boarded the Blue & Gold Fleet for the boat ride out to Alcatraz Island during a visit to San Francisco.

Now, before I start talking about stepping onto The Rock,

here's a bit of tourism advice if you decide to pay a visit to see the place for yourself: buy your tickets in advance. My wife called a phone number provided in a travel guide several days before we left home, and we had our choice of any departure times on the day of our visit. We were told to simply pick the tickets up at a "will call" window there at the departure point.

We had a great time in the City by the Bay, and when our scheduled day came to visit Alcatraz, we parked our car in one of the wharf lots and followed the signs to the Blue & Gold office. It wasn't hard to find – there was a line stretching out from it that must have been fifty yards long. It was snaked out along the walkway, and I couldn't believe how many people were there to buy tickets. I was immediately grateful to my wife for her forethought, since we breezed past all of those people and went to the "will call" window for our tickets. The lady there handed them to us, pointed us toward the wharf, and we were on our way. Remember that little shortcut; it saved us a lot of time. Only those people at the first of the long line got to pick their departure time; everyone else had to take whatever was available.

One more little tip, and I promise that we'll get to Alcatraz. If you're at all prone to motion sickness, be sure to take one of the over-the-counter medications to prepare for the ride over. The water is very choppy, which of course is one of the things that deterred inmates from attempting the swim.

I actually enjoyed the ride, especially getting to view the city from across the bay, and when we arrived at the dock there was a park ranger waiting there with a basic orientation program. He gave us the introduction to our day there, and then dismissed us to watch a film. It was interesting as well, but let's face it – I was ready for The Rock! We looked around the gift shop after the movie, and ran across a fascinating gentleman there at a table: Leon "Whitey" Thompson, the bank robber who spent time at the prison. He was signing copies of his autobiography, *Last Train to Alcatraz*.

A crowd had formed around him, so we hung back until the people dissipated and had moved on with the tour. We had a chance to talk to him, and he turned out to be an interesting fellow. Mr. Thompson calls himself a "retired bank robber," and now spends his time talking to youth groups to try to dissuade them from taking a destructive path like he'd chosen as a young man. I brought up the subject of ghosts as he was signing a book for us, and he smiled at us. As he told us stories of creaking cell doors and footsteps when only the Park staff was present – and no one was in the cellblock – it was hard for me to imagine that this wonderful fellow was once a hardened criminal. The most interesting account that he told was actually seeing a man standing in the cellblock when no one else was supposed to be around. When Whitey approached him, the man slowly faded away into the shadows. It was great to meet Mr. Thompson; not only to hear some first-hand ghost stories, but also to get to shake the hand of a man who had been imprisoned at the Rock, and then turned his life around into being a first-class citizen. I'll never forget Whitey Thompson.

From the gift shop, we made our way up the steep incline that led to the old prison itself, and took a stroll down "Broadway," the central walkway in the cellblock between B and C blocks, toward "Times Square", which is under the clock at the entrance to the cafeteria.

When new prisoners were brought to the prison, they were paraded down Broadway when they first arrived to the taunts of the other prisoners looking out of their cells. Since visiting with Mr. Thompson put us a few minutes behind the crowd, we were able to walk it alone, and the sound of our footsteps sounded eerie, echoing off the concrete and steel. We were later told that when the place is quiet after the public has gone, the park workers have reported strange sounds echoing through the empty building, especially in the area of Broadway: coughs, laughs, whistles, the playing of a harmonica, and even the slamming of cell doors.

The tour was interesting, and we visited every corner of the prison. One particular place of interest was the cafeteria. Warden Johnston, who oversaw the facility from 1933 to 1948, knew that his institution would be housing some of the most dangerous men in America. He also knew that many prison riots had been started because of the poor quality of prison food, so he wanted to make the Alcatraz cafeteria one of the best in the system. He accomplished that feat; the menu was diverse, and prisoners dined on salads, fresh fruit, tasty entrees, and desserts. I'd heard that sounds had also been reported in the cafeteria, such as hushed whispers, the clanking of utensils on trays, and other things that would have been common when the place was in use. While we were there, however, all we could hear were our own voices, and of course, our footsteps. It seemed like there were always footsteps echoing through the halls of the prison.

We also found the hospital entrance – a flight of stairs leading up a floor. Twenty-eight inmates died on Alcatraz: eight resulting from prison fights, five who took their own lives, and fifteen who died from illness in the prison hospital. While we didn't get to visit the hospital itself, we stopped at the stairway leading up to it. With everything still, there was a very strange feeling in the air. I would have loved to climb those steps and walk into the hospital itself – just to see how it felt up there.

Not being one to break the rules, though, we didn't cross the chain, and instead continued on the tour. Different parts of Alcatraz had very different feelings to them, but I think that the strangest place that we visited were the solitary confinement cells. There are more tales of paranormal activity associated with solitary confinement cell 14 than anywhere else on the Rock. The inmates called solitary confinement "the hole", because there was only one small window in the door, which could be closed to seal off the cell completely. The single light was supposed to remain on, but was often turned off by the guards to intimidate the prisoner further. A hole in the floor was used for a toilet, and other than that, the cell was bare. There are rumors of suicides taking place in cell 14, along with the sighting of glowing eyes in the darkness of the cell. It was the only place where we felt anything odd at Alcatraz during our visit. There was one particular place in the cell where both my wife and I separately felt light-headed and a little dizzy; the room seemed to be moving around us.

Before leaving The Rock I had the opportunity to visit with several members of the park staff. Some just rolled their eyes when I asked about hauntings, but others freely shared the information that they had.

I was reflecting on our visit as the Blue & Gold Fleet boat took my wife and me back to San Francisco. I had some very strange feelings at a few places in the tour – mostly a tingly sensation that let me know something odd was going on. It was also interesting to hear some of the first-hand stories. Looking back, I have no doubt that Alcatraz houses a few ghosts from its history. More than that, though, it was a fascinating place to visit. I knew that I would return to San Francisco someday, and that visit would definitely include another trip out to The Rock.

Contact: Alcatraz Island National Park Service, Golden Gate National Recreation Area, Fort Mason, B201, San Francisco, CA 94123. http://www.nps.gov/alcatraz/ .

Author Mitchel Whitington's biography can be found on page 70.

Photo courtesy of the St. Mary's County Historical Society

Touch At Your Own Risk - 1858

Old Jail Museum, Leonardtown, MD

by Jackie Taylor Switzer

An 875-pound boulder, reputedly haunted, sits beside the 1858 Old Jail Museum at Leonardtown, Maryland. It bears a mysterious set of hand and knee impressions. Visitors are allowed to place their hands where the hapless victim's once rested, but many people have reported feeling ill and experiencing aches and pains when they so much as stand near the rock. Some say their cameras malfunction when they attempt to photograph it.

Leonardtown lies about 50 miles south of Washington, D.C. in St. Mary's County. Previously known as Newton, then Seymour Town, before settling on the name Leonardtown, it was the first town incorporated in the United States and has one of the few remaining town squares in Maryland. The jail was built on the lawn of the Courthouse in 1858 and remained in use as a jail until 1942.

Leonardtown was more accessible by boat than by highway until 1910. Tradition says sailing vessels carried peaches to Baltimore and, when they had no return load, would carry granite as ballast on their way back. This granite was used to build the first jail, a one-story building in Leonardtown containing two cells and a hallway. When it became apparent the jailer needed accommodations nearby, the county used bricks from an existing out-building to add a second story on the original granite jail.

Exposed wood lintels over the windows and doors indicate the building was to be covered with stucco later. The jailer and his family used the first floor for their living quarters. The living room, dining room, and kitchen were in the south room, and the bedroom was in the north room. Three jail cells were on the second floor. The large north cell was used for black men, white men in the southeast cell, and women in the small cell on the southwest side. Food was passed to the prisoners through small openings in massive wooden doors that opened into each cell. Since there was little crime in St. Mary's County, the jail came into use mostly for overnight stays rather than long-term criminal detention.

After a new facility was built in 1942, the sturdy old jail served as a county office building and, later, as the offices of the Welfare Department. While refurbishing the jailhouse, the Historical Society discovered the original structure had been taken apart and rebuilt in 1876. Since 1971, St. Mary's County Historical Society Headquarters has occupied the building and operated the Old Jail Museum.

The museum's most intriguing tale dates from colonial days, before the jail was even thought of. Moll Dyer was an eccentric woman with a mysterious past. It was rumored she fled her heritage as an Irish noblewoman with Royal Lineage.

English settlers arrived in Leonardtown around 1635 and in 1649 passed an "Act Concerning Religion," generally known as the Toleration Act. The Toleration Act granted religious freedom to all who believed in God. Moll possibly immigrated to Leonardtown during this time. She lived as an impoverished recluse in a small cabin outside town, gathering herbs and concocting remedies to cure various ailments of the townspeople.

The colony of Maryland mirrored the religious controversies and political upheavals occurring in England at this time. The unrest eventually led to the Protestant Revolution of 1689-1692, and the Toleration Act was voided.

Meanwhile, Leonardtown suffered droughts, crop failures, empty fishing nets, and many other hardships over the years. Seeking a source to blame for all their misfortunes, the townspeople eventually chose Moll Dyer. Her isolated way of living, shadowed past, and reputation as an herbalist drew suspicion among the locals who labeled her a witch and wanted her banned from the town. The Hanover Historical Texts Project has many references to witches from the mid-1400s, leading to the American Colonies' hysteria of the Salem witch trials that ran their course in 1692-3. (Hanover College, Hanover, Indiana. http://history.hanover.edu/project.html)

Five years later, Moll Dyer suffered the consequences of a similar, more local, hysteria. In the winter of 1697 a "pestilence," now thought to have been an epidemic of influenza, swept through the area exacting a heavy death toll. When all the children of the town became ill, Moll Dyer was deemed the cause, and the townspeople set out to kill her. Her neighbors burned down her cabin and drove her into the wilderness on the coldest night of the year.

Terrified, Moll ran from the vigilante group wearing only her housedress, and no winter wrap. They chased her to a large rock where she suddenly stopped and knelt down. Placing one hand on the huge rock and raising the other hand toward the sky, Moll prayed and pronounced a curse upon the land and her persecutors. The townspeople abandoned her to the elements and turned back toward their warm homes. The next morning, ice covered the ground and Moll Dyer was found, frozen to death. She still clutched the giant stone where her hand and knees left permanent impressions. These impressions are everlasting reminders of Moll's fate and the curse she invoked. It is said that bad luck forever followed the residents who set the fire.

It has been over three hundred years since Moll Dyer died. Yet people still report seeing a ghostly apparition floating over the land where she lived, sometimes fleeing as if being chased. The land where Moll's cabin was burned remains barren to this day.

In 1975 the mysterious boulder bearing her hand and knee impressions was moved to be put on display in front of the Old Jail Museum where a large magnolia tree stands as a sentinel. Many museum visitors who touch or photograph the rock take back an experience to remember.

The town that once called Moll Dyer a "witch" and rejected her presence now shares her story and spirit with visitors. Perhaps you will be fortunate enough to attend a performance of "Legend of the Witch, Moll Dyer," a seasonal presentation by the St. Mary's Ballet. The old Jail Museum in historic Leonardtown, Maryland, is an excellent place to start your exploration of the town and, perchance, meet the spirit of Moll Dyer.

Today, the Old Jail Museum provides resources for research, and treats visitors to colorful local folklore, including stories of life in a 19th century jail. It can be found on the town square, at 41625 Courthouse Drive, Leonardtown, Maryland 20650, and is open Wed.- Fri., 12 AM - 2 PM or by special appointment. FFI: 301-475-2467 or contact Susan Erichsen: 301-475-2467 or www.smchistory.org/

The author greatly appreciates the generous access to

information by the following: "The Legend of Moll Dyer: A witch in St. Mary's County, Maryland" by Shelly Beard that was collected as part of a project of "Ghosts and Magicians in Performance," a course in the University Honors Program at the University of Maryland, College Park, taught by David Schlossman, Ph.D. Information on this program can be accessed at www.wam.umd.edu/~dschloss. "History of the Old Jail" by Charles Fenwick. http://smchistory.org/index.htm.

Jackie Taylor Switzer graduated from Texas Woman's University with a BS In Nursing. She is wife, mother, former Girl Scout volunteer, and trauma nurse. She is also a freelance writer and teaches memoir writing classes for Senior University in Georgetown, Texas. Jackie has traveled extensively and pursued her varied interests including genealogy, quilting, photography, cooking, and needlework. All her interests are fodder for her writing. Her articles have appeared in various newsletters and on several internet sites. She has also published in the anthology, *Noble Generation II*, as well as magazines: *Reader's Digest*, *Journal of Emergency Nursing*.

Frank James slept here. Photo courtesy of Jackson County Missouri Historical Society's Jail, Marshall's Home, and Museum

Show Me - 1859

Jackson County Jail, Independence, MO

by Mary Fenoglio

Missouri is known as the "show-me" state, implying that its residents are practical, logical, skeptical folks, not at all the sort to believe in ghosts. Sometimes, however, even the most skeptical among us must admit things happen that defy understanding and hint at a world just beyond our grasp. In certain places the veil seems thin between our everyday lives and other lives unfinished. Often these places are the scene of some old tragedy, a terrible act of violence or just intolerable misery.

The old Jackson County Jail, in Independence, is one such

place. What better avenue for restless souls to express their outrage at the treatment they received there?

Independence lies near the western edge of Missouri, on the south bank of the Missouri River, a suburb now of Kansas City. That whole area is ripe for ghosts from the past, having been under the influence of the Missouri and Osage Indians, the Spanish and the French before becoming American territory with the Louisiana Purchase. How much blood was spilled there in the early days, no one can possibly say. But the misery and bloodshed of the Civil War years in Jackson County is well documented.

The old Jackson County Jail was built in 1859, 12 dungeon-like limestone cells that housed thousands of prisoners from its opening until it closed in 1933. The cells are six feet by nine feet, with two-foot thick walls, one small grated window and a solid iron door. There are six cells upstairs and six downstairs, and there used to be an iron staircase leading to the second floor. The only source of light during the daytime came from the small windows set high in the walls; at night a kerosene lamp was lit in the hallway. It must have been damp and chilly all the time, as cheerless as a grave.

Prior to the Civil War, prisoners were mostly ordinary citizens, arrested for committing a variety of crimes. While some misdemeanors are obvious, like horse racing in the streets and disturbing the peace, building a privy without a pit would seem to be a crime against oneself and therefore to be avoided, jail sentence or not. Other common offences were using firearms in the town limits, disturbing a religious service, and the like.

The advent of the war changed all that. Kansas and Missouri became bitter enemies when Kansas chose to enter the Union as a free state while Missouri remained sympathetic to the south and slavery. War came to the two neighboring states five years before it was actually declared, with guerilla raids and retaliatory killings, the burning of homes and widespread looting.

The jail played a major role in the dissension and disorder. Marshals were commissioned with the duty of keeping order in the face of guerilla raids along the Kansas Missouri border. William Clark Quantrill, leader of a bloody band of pro-Confederate guerillas, was arrested and imprisoned in the Jackson County jail, though he was soon released through the good offices of his friends. The marshal later declared that he had not actually arrested Quantrill, but had only held him in protective custody.

Frank James, the brother of Jesse, also spent time in the jail in 1882. After Jesse was killed, Frank entered into negotiations with the governor of Missouri to surrender, fearing that he would also be murdered. He spent almost six months as a guest in the limestone jail, charged with the crime of murder. However, his southern sympathies accorded him special privileges such as nightly card games and visiting freely with other inmates, and his cell sported a Brussels carpet, fine furniture and paintings on the walls. He was acquitted of the charges against him and lived out his life in the Independence area.

The tables turned when a Union garrison occupied the jail in 1861, the first year of the Civil War. The Union Provost Marshals were nicknamed "Little Gods" because of the power they held over the local citizens. Any supporter voicing southern sympathies was instantly arrested and imprisoned. Cells built to hold three prisoners, claustrophobic enough, often housed more than 20. The cramped cells were often so jammed with prisoners that there was no room for any of them to lie down. A loyalty oath was demanded of citizens; those refusing were jailed, as were those who refused to disclose the whereabouts of members of their families considered to be southern sympathizers. People were murdered randomly, often while trying to obey the Union orders.

Many of the prisoners at that time were women and children, held in the dank, inhumanly overcrowded cells on the charge of harboring guerilla forces. Exactly how young children accomplished the act of harboring anything but a pet cat is unclear, and in any case there was nowhere else for the children to go when their mothers were imprisoned. Their childhoods were forfeit to the fortunes of a war they never made.

In 1901 the old jail was expanded with the addition of a two-story brick building designed to hold minimum-security prisoners. The majority of these were members of so-called "chain gangs" who went out to work every day on roads and other projects, always closely guarded by security officers and wearing shackles on their legs. They left at sunrise every morning, not returning until sunset, six days a week, and they certainly understood the phrase "hard labor." Many of them were sentenced to the chain gangs for relatively minor infractions of the law.

Small wonder that a place of such suffering would have its spirits. The jail is now a museum owned and operated by the Jackson County Historical Society. Both visitors to the jail and staff of the Historical Society have reported feelings of nausea and chills upon entering the old jail and passing one of the first cells. There are also reports of hearing the sound of footsteps, growls and gasps, and the figure of a man in blue has been seen in the cell.

There are two theories about the identity of this man in blue. Marshall Jim Knowles lived in the adjoining marshal's house and lost his life during the Civil War while trying to break up a fight between two prisoners who had opposing views on the war. The other possibility is a deputy marshal who was killed during a jailbreak in June, 1866. Apparently the features of the man have never been seen clearly enough to distinguish his identity.

It is also said that the jail is haunted by the women and

children who were held there during the Civil War. The sounds of children are often heard and apparitions of women and children have been seen. Unexplained occurrences are common to both staff and guests; radios apparently turn on and off by themselves and things are moved around independent of human hands. Perhaps the restless shades of children held captive in that awful place are playing at mischief now in ways they could not do in their lost childhoods.

Feelings of apprehension and ominous dread that are said to come over visitors entering the old building are also said to disappear as swiftly when the limestone walls are exited

Many have no doubt that the old limestone jail is haunted by the wraiths of those who spent such miserable hours locked in its depths, helpless and hopeless against their jailors, guilty only of being in the wrong place at the wrong time.

The jail is now owned and operated by the Jackson County Historical Society, which maintains the buildings and grounds as the 1859 Jail, Marshall's Home and Museum, located at 217 North Main Street, Independence, Missouri. Visitors can take guided tours and self-guided tours of the old jail and the attached Marshall's home. FFI: 816-252-1892; www.jchs.org.

Photo by Mark Ashley

Mary Fenoglio, aka "Gigi", lives on a farm in Central Texas with her husband, happily surrounded by grown children, grandchildren, and an extensive menagerie of birds and animals. She began writing at the age of six in a Big Chief tablet and has kept at it in one form or another for most of her life. A member of Science Fiction and Fantasy Writers of America, she has had stories published in anthologies edited by the late Marion Zimmer Bradley as well as poems published in several magazines. Mary currently writes a weekly column about rural life called “Eggs in My Pocket” for the *Williamson County Sun*, a local newspaper.

Ghosts Of Fort Delaware - 1859
Fort Delaware State Park, Delaware City, DE

by Maureen Timm

"As the long procession of prisoners staggered out upon the wharf at Fort Delaware, the universal thought was one of despondency, as if each had been warned, like the lost spirits of Dante's Hell, 'Abandon Hope, all ye who enter here!' The reputation of the place for cruelty was already familiar to all of us and it needed no more than a glance at the massive fort with its hundred guns, the broad moat, the green slime dykes and scores of sentries pacing to and fro in all directions to quench every lingering hope of escape." (as quoted by Fort Delaware Society)

So wrote Second Lieutenant Randolph Abbot Shotwell, a Confederate veteran from North Carolina, about Fort Delaware, a mosquito-infested prison camp on a marshy piece of ground called Pea Patch Island in the middle of the river separating Delaware from New Jersey.

According to legend, several hundred years ago a boat carrying peas and stones was grounded on a shoal in the middle of the river. Soon the cargo of peas sprouted, took root and formed the beginnings of the island that has since grown to its present size. The Union fortress dates back to 1859. It was originally built to protect passenger and cargo ships arriving in the ports of Wilmington and Philadelphia.

Initially, no one thought of using Fort Delaware as a prison, but in the earliest days of the Civil War, decision makers in the U.S. War Department decided that the fort's isolated island location was ideal for use as a prison. Also, this island site had once been a cemetery for soldiers who died of typhus and malaria. Visitors have seen ghostly images wandering about in the area where the cemetery was once located.

In April 1862, 258 Confederate prisoners, many from Virginia, became the first of 33,000 Southern soldiers who would eventually be imprisoned on the Delaware River island. Since the fort was not built for use as a prison, the first captives were housed in rooms with little ventilation that had been built as powder magazines to hold ammunition. These sites eventually became known as the "dungeons." However, as more POW Rebels arrived, the inside of the fort was overflowing with prisoners, and new facilities were constructed in the marshy wetlands of the islands. These wooden shanties provided little heat in the damp winters—the prisoners had one stove for every 200 men—and poor ventilation during the humid summers. By the summer of 1863, immediately following the Battle of Gettysburg, up to 13,000 Confederate prisoners were held captive at one time. According to some records, approximately 2,700 prisoners died at Fort Delaware: 7 shot, 11 drowned, and the rest succumbed to the ravages of sickness and disease.

Visitors at the fort are given a brochure entitled "Prison Camp Trail." This brochure states that Dr. W. Weir Mitchell, a Philadelphia surgeon who visited the fort in July 1863, when it was most crowded, described the conditions as "an inferno of detained Rebels."

Because of the high water table, very few of the dead were buried on Pea Patch Island. Instead, 2,436 deceased Confederate soldiers were transported on the "death boat" to what is now known as Finn's Point National Cemetery in New Jersey. Their names are listed at the base of a tall monument, but they rest in unmarked graves.

Many Rebels, deciding they had nothing to lose, tried to leave the island before they were sealed in a six foot wooden box. An unknown number, perhaps more than a thousand, escaped or died trying to do so. Some hid in coffins or disguised themselves as Yankee guards. Others made rafts of driftwood, used canteens as floats or stole small boats. And—perhaps the most desperate method—some slipped through privy holes and swam toward the river and freedom, or a drowning death.

The Pentagon-shaped structure covers about six acres of the 70 considered solid, firm land in the 19th century. The parade ground, originally more than two acres, was reduced in 1896 when concrete emplacements for three 12-inch disappearing guns were built in the southern half of the enclosure. The entire east barracks and a portion of the west barracks were removed at that time.

The 32-foot-high walls are of solid granite blocks and bricks and vary in thickness from 7 feet to 30 feet. The fort is surrounded by a 30-foot-wide moat, crossed by a drawbridge on the southwest side leading to the sally port, or principle entrance.

Some of the prisoners held here included British sailor privateers, accused of trying to run the blockade. Most of the ghosts seen here come from the Civil War period. Human pain and misery, violence, survivor guilt, and death in such a place often produces restless spirits that can't let go of this world and enter the next.

Park personnel and tourists have seen ghostly images, felt cold places, and heard voices. On a recent "ghost tour," visitors actually saw the image of a Confederate soldier watching them from the upper ramparts. In the Fort Delaware dungeons people have heard moaning, and the sounds of clanking chains, from the prisoners held here long ago in unpleasant conditions. Under the ramparts and the parade grounds, fleeing Confederate soldiers have been spotted, perhaps an emotional imprint of a failed escape attempt.

In 1985 a visitor snapped a picture of a see-through Confederate Officer standing in an archway. After all these years, is he still being held as a prisoner of war, unable to cross to the other side?

It seems pirates who roamed the island long before the Civil War, in the 1600s and 1700s, also are hanging around the fort. A park ranger was quite surprised one day to see a pirate, dressed in a beautiful green silk shirt and white silk pants, looking out a window at the fort. Pirate spirits must be quite confused at finding a fort on "their" island hideaway.

Pirates were some of the original "snowbirds." When the weather started cooling off the ports of Boston, New York, and Philadelphia, the pirates began making their way south, some taking ships all along the route as far south of St. Vincent just west of Barbados in the Windward Islands of the West Indies.

Here Blackbeard and Hornigold, another pirate, captured the French ship Concorde out of Nantes, France. At that time, Hornigold retired from piracy and Blackbeard re-named the ship the infamous "Queen Anne's Revenge." It is assumed that he was sailing with privateer ships operating out of Jamaica during Queen Anne's War, thus the name "Queen Anne's Revenge."

Cruel and boisterous, the colorfully clad buccaneers so terrorized the shores from New York to the Carolinas that at least one historian hints that the bad memories have been swept under the rug while "other 'nice' occurrences" are remembered and celebrated. The pirate raids are just another part of history that the citizens wish to forget.

We can only imagine a personal confrontation. Hissing through his teeth, Blackbeard, one of the most dreaded pirates who ever lived, jumps to the deck of a merchant ship. He stands tall and lean. Pieces of rope burn like fuses among coils of his black hair. Sashes stuffed with pistols and daggers crisscross his huge chest. Black ribbons flap from the braids in his beard.

But despite his diabolic public image, Blackbeard was an incurable romantic, and when he fell in love, he would usually propose marriage, which was solemnized on the deck of his ship by the first mate. He left no less than 14 brides waiting on shore.

But where did he leave his treasures? When he died, that secret died too. When he had been asked the whereabouts of the fortunes he had collected, he replied, "Only the devil and me know! The longest liver takes all!"

Park rangers feel Blackbeard is still roving the area, keeping an eye on his treasure. Pea Patch Island, after all, would have made a good hiding place; isolated, reachable only by boat, near his favorite territory. Maybe he is trying to outlive the devil so he can "take all."

It is not surprising that lost souls still linger on Pea Patch Island. Suffering went along with being held captive here, and some people were shot at the fort. Prisoners often arrived in terrible shape and frequently starved to death on the premises. Among army personnel, prisoners, and pirates, Pea Patch Island is crowded with persistent spirits.

Some believe that countless restless spirits, who were unable to return to the familiar soil of their Southern homeland, still roam the coastline of Delaware. On dark, misty nights, men in wet, gray uniforms have been seen in the alleyways of Delaware City, along the waterfronts of the coastal towns of New Jersey, and in the reeds and brush of the Pea Patch Island wetlands. Frustrated, these unsettled specters appear lost and weary from years of seeking the eternal rest that they have never found.

The State of Delaware acquired the fort from the federal government in 1947. The Fort Delaware Society, seeking to restore the fort, organized work parties who spent hundreds of hours cleaning, and painting, and re-pointing brick. By 1951 the Society's continuing lobbying efforts paid off as the Delaware legislature declared Fort Delaware a State Park and the officers of the Society as official advisors to the Department of Natural Resources and Environmental Control on the care and maintenance of Fort Delaware State Park.

June, 2005 marked the ninth year of the State Park's evening Ghost/ History Tours. What began as a test program, on Friday the 13th, June 1997, turned into an annual institution, teaching history by luring those interested in the supernatural onto Pea Patch Island and guiding the visitors through the fortress prison.

Several members of the tours have reported seeing a figure wearing a black cloak and carrying a lantern along the second-level restricted corridors.

Prior to one of the season's later tours, Dale Fetzer, one of the Fort Delaware State Park staff, related a story he was told about the "Headless Major." The tale goes that an old caretaker of the fort used to stop in at a local Delaware City gin mill after his shift. On one evening he came in terrified and shaking. He said he saw a "Headless Major," dressed in a Confederate uniform roaming the ramparts.

Getting to the Park is an adventure in itself. From the parking area in Delaware City, visitors take a half-mile ferry ride to Pea Patch Island aboard the Delaware River and Bay Authority's Three Fort Ferry. A jitney provides transportation from the island dock to the granite and brick fortress. Here, authentically-clad historical interpreters begin your journey back to the summer of 1863.

Fort Delaware State Park is open weekends and holidays from late April through September and Wednesdays through Sundays from mid-June until Labor Day. The park is closed Mondays and Tuesdays with the exception of holidays on those weekdays. FFI: Fort Delaware State Park, P. O. Box 170,,Delaware City, DE 19706. Contact them by phone: 302-834-7941 or check the website: www.del.net/org/fort.

Maureen Timm has been a freelance writer since 1995 and currently writes for newspapers and *Antiques & Collectibles* magazine. She started writing for the Neighbors section in the

Sun Herald in 2002. She received her Bachelors Degree in Business Administration from the University of Colorado in Boulder and was also an ASID Associate and owned and operated her design studio named Angel's Interiors in Fort Myers, Florida. She is a member of the Gulf Coast Writers Association, The Hancock County Historical Society, and Pass Christian Art Association.

Photo courtesy of Gilpin Historical Society and Museums

Ghosts Of Gold Rush Days - 1862

Washington Hall Jail, Central City, CO

by Ann Alexander Leggett

In the late 1800s, the wild, wild West lived up to its name in Central City, Colorado. Located in the Rocky Mountains, 35 miles west of Denver, the sleepy little town awoke to the gold rush when John H. Gregory discovered gold outside the city limits of Central City and its neighboring town of Black Hawk in 1859. Lured by riches, men clamored to lay claim to any piece of available ground. Within days the news of the gold strike reached Denver, and two months later Central City boomed as a mining town and home to 10,000 people.

A report prepared by the Gilpin County Historical Society pretty much sums up the colorful town and its residents.

"Those who settled in Central City were never hard up for wild times. In 1861 alone, Central City recorded 217 fistfights, 97 revolver fights, 11 Bowie knife fights and one dogfight. And amazingly, no one was killed." But with its burgeoning population, worse crimes were committed and it soon became apparent that Central City needed a jail.

Talk to most Central City historians and they will say that Washington Hall, the home of the first jail, is one of the town's oldest structures and the certainly the oldest continuously used public building in the state. Sheriff William "Billy" Cozens built Washington Hall in 1862, but his wife Mary York was actually the driving force behind the new jail. Apparently tired of her sheriff-husband handcuffing inmates to the furniture in her home for lack of secure facilities, she put her foot down, and the jail finally became a reality with the blessing of the Board of Gilpin County Commissioners.

Not only was Cozens the local sheriff, but a trained carpenter as well. He personally set about constructing the jail using hand-hewn logs and stone to construct the walls, and on March 1, 1862, he welcomed his first prisoners. The jail held six to eight inmates at a time, too many for the 12- x 5-foot jail cell, and conditions were less than satisfactory. By 1864 Cozens had expanded the little jail to include a second story, which over the years, was used as a public meeting place, a courthouse, a firehouse, and additional jail space.

These days the tales of ghosts roaming Central City and its jail make their way around town. People tell about spirits of those who perhaps paid the ultimate price for their crimes or died from the effects of brutal weather while merely waiting to be sentenced.

In 1948 the Gilpin County Art Association moved into some of the upstairs offices, and in 1996, Don Harvey, a structural engineer by trade, agreed to install a hydraulic elevator in the downstairs cell space as a favor to his wife, who was at the time the president of the Association. He had heard stories about hauntings but never took them seriously. The downstairs "jail room" itself had been empty for quite some time. When he first entered, he could immediately imagine the harsh living conditions endured by the prisoners. "The outside wall was stone," he said, "and I could see daylight through the cracks. With Central City's cold winters, the men must have been miserable."

One wall was made of 10-inch diameter logs, shored up with old wood and steel plates. The dirt floors sloped and a wood stove, black with soot, still stood just outside the jail door near the stairs where the guards sat to keep warm. Five wooden bunks, simply framed boxes, still hung on the walls, and bits of shredded newspaper and pieces of faded long johns were meticulously stuffed into the cracks between the stones, reminders of the 15 to 20 degree-below-zero winters common in these hills.

Along with two jackhammer workers, who were miners from the nearby Henderson Mine, Don set to work preparing the site for the elevator. The work was backbreaking as the men tore through the old logs and stone and rebuilt the walls. The marred steel plates and the old steel door were removed. Despite their exhaustion at the end of each workday, the men began to wonder who was playing a trick on them with the lights.

"Every night when we left, we would turn off the lights," Don said, "and every morning they would be on when we came back into the room. The strange thing was that I was the only one with a key to that space. Finally we began to question each other: 'Did you forget to turn the light off last night?' That sort of thing. Finally, at the end of each day we'd all stand around the light switch and witness turning it off. And sure enough, when we'd come back in the morning, they'd be on again. Finally we realized that whatever was in there didn't like being in the dark so we left the lights on every night."

Don and his crew had felt the presence of something in the

jail from the beginning but now it seemed certain that the stories they had heard were true. "We started talking to the spirits, which we felt were the ghosts of men who had died in the jail," Don said. "We would tell them that we were sorry they had to endure such tough conditions. But we also wanted them on our good side. We didn't want them to make our job difficult or take our tools."

The hauntings didn't stop there. One day on a whim, one of the jackhammer operators decided to lie down in one of the bunks before they were torn off the walls, to see firsthand just how uncomfortable they must have been. His experience was not pleasant.

"He couldn't get out," Don said. "He felt something grip his shirt and pull him down and he was finally able to wrestle free and jump out of the bunk." The bunks came down quickly after that.

The men went on to finish the job, mindful that they were not alone in the old jail and respectful of the spirits that still seem to linger. And apparently the Art Association employees still hear things that are a bit out of the ordinary such as voices in the old cell space near the elevator and footsteps on the stairs leading up to the gallery even after the building has been closed for the day. The jail had been unused and doors were sprung many, many years ago, yet it still seems the ghosts in Central City's Washington Hall are resolutely imprisoned.

Today Washington Hall still houses the Art Association gallery and the City Manager's Office. The City Council continues to meet in the building as well. Visitors are welcome to walk through the building and see the gallery at 117 Eureka Street, Central City, CO; Art Association phone: 303-582-5952.

Things that go bump in the night have always intrigued Ann Alexander Leggett, who is the co-author of two ghost books about Boulder, Colorado: *Haunted Boulder, Ghostly Tales From the Foot of the Flatirons*, and *Haunted Boulder 2,*

Ghostly Tales From Boulder and Beyond. But, she says, it is the history behind the haunted structures that makes a good ghost story. As a result, her tales weave historical facts with eerie spiritual encounters. Ann's books may be found at: www.whitesandlakepress.com.

In between ghost stories, she continues her work as a freelance publication designer/desktop publisher, artist, manager of two teenagers (one in college, one at home). She spends any extra time learning to surf (not in Colorado), biking, rowing, and managing the Colorado Junior Crew program, a high school rowing program in Boulder founded by her son.

Photo courtesy of www.ohiotrespassers.com

Gothic Prison - 1866

Moundsville State Penitentiary, Moundsville, WV

by Elizabeth J. Baldwin

Built in 1866, at the height of the Gothic Revival style of architecture in America, Moundsville State Penitentiary looks like a Transylvanian castle, complete with turrets and battlements, created in the best horror film tradition. Moundsville is located in West Virginia's panhandle, a mere 30-mile wide finger of the state separating Pennsylvania and Ohio. Moundsville State Penitentiary now serves as a center for community activities. You may see a dog training class going on in the former prisoners' exercise yard, while nearby seniors play bingo—or a tour guide conducts a mock hanging. Prisoners from a nearby minimum-security facility also make up part of the scene, restoring and maintaining the grounds.

But according to reports from many visitors and staff, at night the scene is likely to change. This facility is billed as one of the *Most Haunted Prisons in America* and has been featured on MTV *Fear* and the Learning Channel. SciFi's "Proof Positive" even filmed a ghost hunter trying to use equipment to prove the existence of ghosts.

You may see a phantom guard making his rounds on the battlements as he keeps a watchful eye over the prisoners, even though there hasn't been a resident prisoner or guard here since 1995. If you listen closely enough, you can hear the clash and clang of the special gate in the North building known as the Wagon Gate, as if ghostly prisoners are being admitted to serve their time. The North building, the first one raised on the 10-20-acre complex, has the most reported spectral activity, other than the Sugar Shack.

The Sugar Shack is considered the "hot spot." Located in the basement this was used as an indoor recreation room during bad weather. Left pretty much to their own devices in this room, the prisoners and their activities left behind a palpable aura of fear and violence.

Visitors on tours sometimes report hearing a water fountain being used after they've passed it—only the fountain was unplugged in 1995 and hasn't been plugged back in since. There's a sound of keys rattling and cell doors clashing and clanging as if being opened and closed. Screams and footsteps may come to your ears even though nobody is around except those on the tour. Occasionally people report seeing the ghostly outlines of people going about their business in the old prison, or even reenacting old crimes committed in these dank cells and halls. Dark graffiti adds to the negative atmosphere. Some visitors are so overcome with emotion they have to be helped from cell number 17 on death row. This was a condemned man's last cell before he was executed.

The ghost most often reported is that of a trustee who was murdered in the basement. Prisoners and guards alike had used him to transfer information. When new prisoners didn't understand this trustee's role in prison life, they regarded him as a "snitch." They cornered him in the bathroom and stabbed him to death with homemade knives. The hapless trustee still wanders that area. Is he confused about why he was attacked?

Death row, or the Alamo, as it was known by those who resided there, not surprisingly, harbors eerie sensations left behind by the prisoners executed at Moundsville. From 1899 until 1949, 85 men met their demise at the end of a rope. One prisoner was decapitated when his 200-pound-plus body proved too heavy for his neck to hold. After 1954 "Old Sparky," as they called the electric chair, became the method of execution, and nine more prisoners died before West Virginia abolished the death penalty in 1965.

Moundsville has a lengthy record of incidents to lend credence to its claim of being haunted. Recorded activity ranges from unexplained cold spots to poltergeist activity to ghost sightings. In its time the prison housed some of the most notorious criminals of the day. Prisoners ranged from inmates as vicious as Charles Manson to coal miners arrested and imprisoned for daring to strike for better wages and working conditions. With a concentration of the worst society had to offer, in some of the worst conditions, Moundsville Prison was the site of many horrible crimes. Murder, torture, suicide, rape, as well as numerous deaths by disease took place in the prison over its lengthy history.

A graveyard for those who died and were unclaimed by friends or relatives was located on the South wall side of the prison from 1866 to 1890. It was eventually moved to another location, outside the city limits and is now called Whitegate Cemetery.

But the tragic events generated by a prison population account for only part of the haunted atmosphere surrounding Moundsville. The prison itself was built on the site of an ancient burial ground. Such sites are in and of themselves areas of much ghostly activity. Moundsville takes its name from a nearby large, conical-type Adena Mound. Determined to date back to approximately 250-150 BCE (Before Common Era), it was excavated in 1838. No further detailed archaeological testing has taken place since then. Grave Creek Mound National Historical Site is located across from the prison.

More than 20,000 visitors arrive in Moundsville, West Virginia each year to experience the thrills offered by the now defunct prison. Tour guides check their guests in as if they are prisoners, complete with mug shots. A museum offers a view of "Old Sparky," and also a demonstration of just exactly how hanging worked. Perhaps the most enigmatic item on display is a letter from Charles Manson requesting that he be transferred to Moundsville on the promise that he would cause no trouble. Certain tours specialize in ghost hunts—perhaps with more success than most people want when hunting phantoms. Even night tours are available for those brave at heart.

Happy ghost hunting.

The prison is located at 818 Jefferson Avenue, Moundsville, West Virginia. Follow the signs into downtown Moundsville where the old prison is located. FFI: (304) 845-6200. Those wanting to learn more about Moundsville as one of America's Most Haunted Prisons can go to the website: www.wvpentours.com, and also www.ohiotrespassers.com/mound.html to find the times and kinds of tours offered, as well as to see prison photos.

Elizabeth J. Baldwin is a writer and animal trainer who lives in Central Texas with her husband of 30 years, as well as seven horses, six cats, three dogs, and assorted wild life trying to move up to the good life. Occasionally companion animals that have already crossed the Rainbow Bridge will stop by to check on things.

Elizabeth is currently marketing a paranormal romance about witches and shape shifters. She is also working on a new

Photo by Mary Ann Melton

book—a science fantasy novel about parallel worlds. Author of articles about horsemanship and animal training, she currently has an experimental e-book available at: http://friendlyhorsmanship.com. Readers may contact Ms. Baldwin at: http://journals.aol.com/elizbald/ViewfromtheLiveryString, or ej_baldwin@yahoo.com.

Photo courtesy of Larry and Margaret Stephens

Serve Your Sentence In Style - 1872

Old Washington Jail Bed and Breakfast Inn, Washington, AR

by Alan L. "Buz" Lowe

Today the old part of Washington, Arkansas has been turned into a historic state park, complete with guides costumed in Old South regalia. You too can get into the act and spend a night in the old jail, which is now a bed and breakfast. But don't be surprised if you're checked in by Sheriff Ike, who is serving a self-imposed ghostly sentence for eternity.

The city of Washington, Arkansas, was incorporated in 1824 before Arkansas was a state. It wasn't long before it became the hub of economic and social growth in southwest Arkansas. Washington was the last stop before entering the wild, wild west.

Because of its border proximity, it played an important role in Texas's 1835-36 war for independence from Mexico. While residing in one of the town's taverns in 1834, Sam Houston and others discussed plans for the Texas revolt. Volunteers passed through en route to the Texas battlefields, including frontiersman Davy Crockett, who stayed briefly in late 1835 on his way to his death at the Alamo in March 1836. Another Alamo casualty, Jim Bowie, also visited the town on his way to Texas, and it was there that a blacksmith named James Black is believed to have made the original, famed knife for Bowie in 1830 or 1831.

When Union forces captured Little Rock in 1863, the state's Confederate government relocated to Washington, Arkansas. While the government was located there, they used the 1836 Hempstead County Courthouse as its capitol. This courthouse still exists today but was replaced by a new courthouse in 1874. Washington remained in Confederate hands throughout the war. Because of this fact, the community's fine old structures were protected from damage often caused by occupying armies.

As the city began to decline in the 1870s a new county courthouse and county jail were constructed to help bolster the city's economy and preserve its place as the county seat. The new two-story jail was built in 1872, two years before the courthouse. Both served Hempstead County until 1939 when the county seat was transferred to Hope and a new courthouse and jail were built. The abandoned old jail sat unattended until it was converted into a boarding house in the 40s. It remained such until 1980 when it was converted into a bed and breakfast.

Today, the Washington Jail Bed and Breakfast is owned by Larry and Margaret Stephens. The Stephens have restored the old jail to its original splendor, with some minor changes. Visitors and guests are no longer locked behind bars and made to sleep on hard lumpy beds, but rather a person is treated to luxurious accommodations. Visitors and guests are no longer escorted to their rooms by burly men carrying guns and handcuffs; they are met at the door with a friendly smile and a big Arkansas welcome. Oh, yes, one other thing—they might also be met by the resident ghost.

The Inn is a beautiful old two-story building situated about two blocks from the 1874 Courthouse. The building looks more like an antebellum mansion built for local aristocrats than a county jailhouse. The dining room still has "graffiti" from the original occupants. The walls and ceilings are made of two-foot thick concrete which makes an already tranquil setting quieter. Many guests have commented that their stay was very peaceful, but that is not all they have said about the old jailhouse.

Legend has it that, in 1920, the Sheriff of Nevada County, a neighboring county to the south, was incarcerated and held for trial in the Hempstead County Jail (now the Old Washington Jail Bed and Breakfast Inn). The sheriff was held outside his own county not only because he was arrested at Hempstead County. Also law officials believed that either the local women of Nevada County might lynch him or his deputies might set him free.

It appears that the popular Sheriff Ike had a good life in Nevada County. He had a good wife and good children. But as is the case with some people, the sheriff began to want more than the attentions of his wife, so he turned to his stepdaughter too. In the 20s an extramarital affair was absolutely shameful, but an affair with your step daughter was (and is) unforgivable. The girl got pregnant and nature began to reveal the dark secret she withheld from her mother. When the sheriff's wife, the daughter's mother, found out what had been going on behind her back, she was furious. She confronted the sheriff and a fight followed. Mother and daughter left Ike soon after that. While they waited for a train in Hope, Arkansas, Ike approached them. He did everything he could to stop them from leaving, to no avail. When all else failed, the sheriff drew his gun to stop them from boarding the train. By then the Hope Police and the county sheriff had been summoned to the train station to stop what appeared to be a killing in progress. The sheriff was arrested and hauled off to the Hempstead County lock up to await trial. His sinful ways had caught up with him.

While locked up in the Old Washington Jail in Hempstead County, he had time to think about his crime. He decided that he was a branded man and had little or no hope of a future if released from jail. He feared for his life. Rather than face the ridicule and hopelessness of a failed life he decided to hang himself. One evening after the final cell check, he took his bed sheet, formed a noose and executed the justice he felt he deserved. This was particularly difficult in that there was no furniture from which to jump. He literally choked himself to death. The next morning the Hempstead County Deputy Sheriff found his lifeless body hanging in the cell. The Sheriff of Nevada County, Ike as he has become known, remains in the jailhouse serving a self-imposed sentence of eternity in jail.

He does little things to let the owners know he is still around. Some of the guests have been so frightened by things that they see that they have left in the middle of the night. The sheriff has been seen walking the halls opening and closing doors as if to check on the residence. He never intends to frighten, but it can be unnerving to have a ghost moving about the house. The sheriff likes to move things and even hide them from unsuspecting visitors. Larry, the owner, recalls one evening in particular. He had decided to go to bed early and read. When he retired, he left the book on the night stand. The next morning it was gone. Later the next day, Larry found the book in his car parked in the drive outside the house.

Because of the stories told about this old jail, the owners decided to determine if the stories had any merit. Team one of Spirit Seekers, of which this author is a part, was sent to the city of Washington, Arkansas. We all met at the Bed and

Breakfast around 9 PM. We each had a room and, after getting settled in, we prepared for a long evening. The night started uneventfully but ended with a bang.

Our team psychic, Violet, began by walking around through the house in an effort to determine if and where there was spirit activity. In the Pilkington Room, she felt as if she was not alone. In the Deloney Room, she felt that something very emotional had happened there. She thought maybe there was a residual haunting there. In the Monroe Room, she hit pay dirt.

In this room she met Robert. He was a prisoner who had been convicted but swears he did not commit the crime. While the psychic was communicating with Robert, I saw what appeared to be a shadow of a person standing close to her. There was very little light in the room, but what I saw was a much darker shape on an already dark wall. The remainder of the investigation centered on the Monroe Room, where most of the paranormal data was collected. However, we did manage to gather data throughout the entire house. While there, we collected photographs of spirit energy at rest and in motion. After the equipment was put away and the investigators had retired for the evening, spirit activity increased.

Violet wanted to stay in the Monroe Room and continue trying to communicate with whatever spirits were there. She could feel that the spirit was there but did not want to communicate and this feeling continued all night. I stayed in the Deloney Room, and while I slept soundly enough, I was awakened several times by what felt like a fingers on my face, neck and arm. The feeling was annoying but not threatening in any way.

Terri, one of our trainees, stayed in the Pilkington Room, and she had her eyeglasses taken from her face. Although this frightened her, she said she did not feel threatened. Because she had been frightened, she went out on the front porch to get some air. While out there, she saw one of the three rocking chairs start to rock.

After reviewing the data gathered and listening to the reading of the investigators' reports, we have concluded that the stories concerning the Old Washington Jail Bed and Breakfast do have merit. All of the spirit activity appears to be benign in nature, and from all accounts, Ike made an appearance in the Pilkington Room while Robert stayed put in the Monroe Room.

So, when you visit the Old Washington Jail Bed and Breakfast and see the sheriff walking the halls checking the doors, don't be frightened. He is only doing his job by checking on the visitors and guests to make sure that all is well.

The Old Washington Jail Bed and Breakfast Inn is conveniently located just nine miles north of Hope, Arkansas, on Hwy 278. The address is The Old Washington Jail Bed and Breakfast, Old Washington Historic State Park, Washington, Arkansas 71862; phone: (870) 983-2461; www.theinnkeeper.com/bnb/8156.

Alan Lowe was born, raised, and educated in Little Rock, Arkansas. By trade he is a construction engineer. He became interested in spirits and the spirit world about twelve years ago when he met his wife, Angela, who is spirit sensitive. With her help, he has developed Spirit Seekers Paranormal Research Team. The last few years they have investigated and documented strange occurrences across the south. The team has been invited into private residences, commercial properties, and public facilities.

This group investigates and documents the spirit world and is committed to the research, documentation, education, and investigation of ghostly phenomena recorded through EVP, digital, film and video photography. For any number of reasons, some spirits have elected to stay here or have been anchored here, unable to move on. Spirit Seekers, as a whole, desire the knowledge and understanding of life after death.

One of the main goals is to assist those who are experiencing paranormal phenomenon. Alan and Angela will look for authentic evidence of the paranormal and try to determine if the location is haunted. They do not charge a fee for their services and invite you to contact them at: www.thespiritseekers.org.

Julius Greenwald: Scapeghost - 1872
Wyoming Territorial Penitentiary, Laramie, WY

by Zoey Quinn

The Wyoming Territorial Penitentiary was home to 1,063 men over the course of thirty some-odd years, including Tom Horn and Butch Cassidy – in fact, it was the only prison Butch ever saw the inside of, back in 1893, when he was sent there from Lander, Wyoming for stealing a horse. While this particular hoosegow may not have the most or the meanest ghosts, it sure has one of the most cantankerous.

Dedicated in 1872 to "evil doers of all classes and kinds," the prison was the most massive stone building of its time, an imposing figure looming up out of the vast plains surrounding it. A bottle of "Old Bourbon" was buried beneath the cornerstone, to commemorate the role that the ol' demon whiskey would play in most of the crimes causing incarceration.

Sadly though, just a little over one hundred years later, the ruins of the Laramie prison had become just a crumbling reminder of Wyoming's wild outlaw past. A combination of legislation and fiscal frustration had motivated the state to build a new penitentiary over in Rawlins, so by 1903 most every prisoner was being housed there, and the once impressive structure sat as empty as a tick in a teacup. A few years later, the prison and grounds were turned over to the University of Wyoming for use as a stock farm. They used it all right, for nigh on 60 years, but everything slowly deteriorated until eventually the city of Laramie had seen fit to condemn the rosy-brick structure.

In 1989, some local folks heard opportunity knocking, and raised money to put the old girl back on her feet. Hope was, with some hard work and elbow grease, the "Stone House Across the River" would attract destination tourists as well as folks passing through Laramie on their way to just-about-anywhere else.

Now, rumor had it that the prison was haunted. Stories flew thick and fast in the Wyoming wind, but no one could say for sure. At least not until that summer day when Julius Greenwald decided to show himself.

Some folks say it was the construction noise that brought him out. Others'll tell you he didn't care for strangers traipsing around his cell, and he wanted to give them an earful. There's even some that swear he just had a mean hankering for a decent cigar.

Whatever the reason, in the summer of 1991, the ghost of Julius Greenwald, prisoner #338, scared the dickens out of a couple of tourists from California! Well, instead of going from pillar to post, it's likely best to start right at the beginning, with Julius's flesh and bone arrival at the prison.

Back in the 1890s, Julius was a cigar maker out in Provo. His cigars were as fine as cream gravy, and he had the flannel mouth of a true salesman to boot, but the tobacco business in

Utah was poorly. Religious attitudes thereabouts put a spoke in the wheel when it came to smoking. That being the case, Julius took to traveling the neighboring states to make his sales. Folks in Wyoming liked their smokes the same as they liked their whiskey, strong and often – so Julius knew his way around there as much as anyone.

His first stop in Wyoming was always Evanston, a little town just across the state line. He'd stop there on his way out and on his way home too. Sales were always better farther along, in towns like Cheyenne and Laramie and Sheridan, but Evanston had something those other places didn't, namely, Julius's favorite "house of ill-repute."

Seems he started visiting there a while before he got married, and failed to get out of the habit once he did. ('Course, a person could speculate on where Julius met his bride, Jennie, but anybody who claims to know for sure is a liar, since whoever was there is gone now, one way or another.)

Now, Julius might've sold out his cigars faster than expected on this one particular trip. Or, he might've just missed his Jennie and headed home sooner than expected, but at any rate, Julius found himself there in Evanston on August the 2nd, 1897, knocking on the door of the bordello. Once inside, he came face to face with Jennie, who'd been working there going on a week! Instead of pulling in his horns, Julius pulled out his pistol and shot her dead.

Thirty-eight year old Julius Greenwald was convicted right quick of Murder in the Second Degree. That sentence made him a prisoner of the state and got him a lifetime stay at the Laramie Territorial Prison, 300 miles away from the scene of his crime. He commenced his residency in Laramie just a few weeks later, on September the 29th, 1897.

Julius had never been one for school, but he knew how to make cigars. Since he figured on staying awhile, he convinced prison officials to let him start a cigar factory right there at the penitentiary. And all things being equal, Julius should have had an illustrious career as the prison's cigar manufacturer, but of course all things are rarely equal. Oh, he did spend the rest of his life behind those two-foot-thick limestone walls in Laramie; it's just that "the rest of his life" only amounted to a tad under three and one-half years.

On February 13, 1901, Julius Greenwald died of an "organic heart disease of rheumatic origin." They doctored him right there at the prison, but Julius was pronounced dead at 8 PM. Prison officials sent his body back to Utah, where his people were, but those California tourists'll tell you that the rest of him didn't make it back there. His spirit's not more'n two whoops and a holler from his cell on the third tier of the prison!

Keep in mind that Julius was only the second, and the last, inmate to die while incarcerated in the Wyoming Territorial Prison. The first inmate to die there was shot during a violent prison revolt in 1893. He was ringleader of a gang of six men who jumped a guard and beat the man near to death with his own cane. Being that Julius was the only man to die peacefully behind the walls of the prison maybe helps explain why his spirit would've decided to stick around.

Julius's cell was in the original part of the prison building, known as the North Wing. For the superstitious out there, it's interesting to note that that particular block was constructed with thirteen windows, with each window thirteen feet high and thirteen inches wide. (And if that doesn't walk a goose over your grave, standing there amidst all those architectural "thirteen" measurements will at least get you to feeling mighty unlucky!) Looking over to the center of the building, there was a block of cells, three tiers high, surrounded by an eight-foot wide corridor. Seven cells faced east, and seven cells faced west, back to back, on each level. Most of those cells have been removed, to make room for the sightseers, though they left some whole, so people can get a feel of what it looked like at the start.

I'd best keep the pot boiling and get back to those tourists. It helps though, to get a picture in your mind's eye of just where Julius spent his time, both in body, and later, in spirit. Forty-two cells, each one six feet wide, eight feet deep and only just as high served as home to two prisoners. There wasn't much room to turn around with two canvas sleeping hammocks hanging from the ceiling. Back when Julius first arrived, the prison was dark, dirty and damp, even in the dry heat of a Laramie summer.

But by the summer of 1991, the prison and the surrounding ground had on its best bib and tucker, all spruced up and open for tourist trade. Out-of-towners and locals alike were standing in line to take guided tours of the prison, walk down the Main Street of Frontier Town, and most of all to hear tales about how the law tried to tame the Wild West.

Wyoming gets as hot in the summer as it gets cold in the winter. It was precisely one of those dog-days, mid July and close to noon – the time and type of day that brings out the faint in folks. Even so, when the tour guide looked over at the middle-aged man clutching his wife's arm and staring wide-eyed and wordlessly at something behind her, she knew it was more than the heat. The man's wife knew too. The summer tan was drained from her husband's face and he was white as . . . a ghost.

"Are you all right" she asked? "What's wrong?" His mouth was opening and closing like a trout in the grass.

"Over there…right over there," he stammered, pointing to the doorway of what had been one of the top-most cells. "A man was there. Clear as day. He was reaching out, like this," he said, raising his arms up halfway, palms pointed out. "I saw him. And then he…he just…he disappeared."

Another member of the tour group helped the woman prop her husband up against the wall. He looked frightened. "I saw him too," he said cautiously. "A man. Short. He stood right there, and he stretched out his arms. He looked right at me, and then he was suddenly just gone!"

The tour guide was shaken up a might and high-tailed the men to the Park Director's office to relate what had happened. The two were brought into separate rooms where they sorted through stacks of prisoner's photos. And this here is Simon Pure... both men, on their own and without knowing what the other was doing, picked Prisoner #338, Julius Greenwald, as "the man in the doorway."

Turns out the Park Director wasn't much surprised when both of the men recognized Julius. After all, the incident had taken place right there on the third tier, and according to pre-renovation blueprints, the "doorway" was exactly where Julius Greenwald's cell door had been.

And that's how the scuttlebutt started. These days, Julius has become a "scapeghost" of sorts around the Wyoming Territorial Prison. Minor re-construction of exhibits is on-going, and when a hammer goes missing, especially towards the end of the day, the workmen figure Julius is just aiming to get a bit of peace and quiet. Most of the staff and volunteers no longer look the least bit taken aback when a new visitor, out of the blue, sniffs the air and asks "Where's that cigar smoke coming from?"

"Oh, that's just Julius," they smile, shaking their heads.

And even the still-slightly-skeptical among them will take notice that they too are catching a whiff of cigar smell despite the strictly enforced No Smoking regulations.

Wyoming Territorial Prison is located at 975 Snowy Range Road, Laramie, WY 82073. FFI: (307) 745-6161.

Zoey Quinn – Writing from the comfortable confines of a rehabbed 1967 Airstream trailer (parked somewhere in the Middle of Nowhere, Wyoming), Zoey says, "Life is good." After taking a couple of stabs at Real Jobs (and some not so real), she is ready to take the plunge into pretty-close-to-full-time writing. Or painting. We'll see which way the wind

The author/artist is always on the lookout for the unusual.

blows. Zoey doesn't want to write grants, or paint stage scenery, as each of these falls into the category of Real Jobs Already Stabbed At. Her current project, a picture book for grown-ups, is entitled "The Guilded Turd." You can keep up with how she's moving along at her website: www.zoeyquinn.com.

Old Disciplinary Barracks, photo by Kathy Weiser, www.legendsofamerica.com

An Army Of Ghosts - 1875
Old Disciplinary Barracks, Fort Leavenworth, KS

by Carol MacDonald Menchu

Fort Leavenworth was established by Henry Leavenworth on the Missouri River in May, 1827. The first settlement in the Kansas territory, it is the oldest active Army post west of the Mississippi River. The Fort initially served as a quartermaster depot, arsenal, and troop post, and was dedicated to protecting the fur trade and safeguarding commerce on the Santa Fe Trail.

In 1875, the United States Disciplinary Barracks, which at one time held more than 1,000 prisoners, was established and continued in use until 2002, when a new barracks was built. During World War II it became the temporary home of many German POWs.

This old building has twelve towers along its wall, some of

which were renovated over the years. Five or six towers would be used at a time, depending upon what day of the week it was. By World War II, the door to get into one tower from the ground had been bricked off, had not been renovated, and was never manned. The only way you could get into Eight Tower was to walk along the wall from the number Seven or Nine Tower.

Sometimes a man was seen moving around in Eight Tower. You could never tell who it was, but it caught attention. The legend is that a soldier shot himself in the head with his shotgun in Eight Tower, and that it had never been manned since.

There was no phone in Eight Tower, but the Control Tower would often get phone calls from it. When the line was picked up, there would be only static on the other end.

An M.P. patrol driving down the road next to the barracks saw someone standing in Eight Tower pointing a shotgun at them. They called Control to tell the guard in the Tower to stop pointing his gun at them only to be told there was no one in the Tower.

Seven Tower was also haunted. The sergeant in charge of posting the towers would walk the soldiers around to the towers, unlock a gate, and then unlock the door at the bottom of the tower. From there the on-going guard would walk up a spiral staircase, knock on a trap door, and say the daily password. The off-going guard would then unlock the trap door, and they would switch. The sergeant would then again lock the tower.

One afternoon, the Seven Tower guard radioed there was somebody knocking at the tower door, trying to get in, but when he looked out the window, he couldn't see anyone. The sergeant went to investigate. On his way, another call was heard over the radio saying that somebody was walking up the steps. The sergeant started running toward the tower, knowing backup was on the way. The guard called again, screaming the intruder was banging on the trapdoor, trying to get into the tower while the guard stood on the trap door to keep it shut.

The sergeant could hear the banging on the steel door and hear the guard yelling as he ran up to the tower. The sergeant opened the gate, then opened the door to the tower, and stepped inside. He looked up. The pounding stopped. There was no one was on the steps.

Guards with duty in Four Tower and Six Tower had similar occurrences. They would hear somebody at the bottom of their tower, and thinking it was time to "rotate," they would pack up and get ready to leave. They would hear someone walking up the metal staircase, but no one ever knocked. The guard would eventually open the trap door and no one would be there.

Inside the Disciplinary Barracks walls, Building 65 was the prison hospital. It has an unused elevator that is also said to be haunted. According to legend, 14 prisoners were executed in the elevator shaft by hanging. Often guards would report hearing screaming coming from the old elevator.

It was common knowledge among everyone who worked in Building 65 at night that the top of the elevator shaft had a light that would always stay on. On one occasion a guard went up to the top of the shaft and turned the light off. After locking everything back up, he walked to the courtyard—the light was still off. Coming back through the courtyard about an hour later, the light was back on.

The elevator would also move by itself. You could look through the crack in the doors and see it. Days later when you looked again from the same floor, it would have moved. No one ever said they heard it move.

The third floor of Building 65 was closed off to the inmates by two locked gates and was being used for storage. A ghostly man in a wheelchair was often seen there, being pushed by another ghostly figure. There are stories of inmates walking down to the Guard Cage in the middle of the night. When asked if something was wrong, they would say that the guy in the wheelchair had awakened them.

Inside the Castle, as the Barracks was called, in the wings of the building, an occasional "shadow person" would be seen. While walking on the bottom tier, 3 tier, someone could be seen walking up on 7 or 8 tier. Both 7 and 8 tiers were locked off and being used only for storage. A check of personnel would reveal all guards accounted for, all inmates locked down, and the tiers locked.

Guards were not allowed to smoke inside the walls of the Castle, and would walk to the back of the tiers and up to 7 or 8 tier, to sit on the steps and smoke their cigarettes. One guard would be in the guard cage with two others sitting right across from each other, and they would hear someone walking up the stairs. When they checked to see who it was, no one was there.

Sometimes, the guards would take short naps during their break, but one would always stay awake, in case someone called over the radio. Two guards told of dreaming of a man, possibly a soldier, in an olive drab uniform, walking the tiers. This man would walk up to them and tap them on the shoulder, waking them up. The guard who was awake all the time never saw anyone.

The old Disciplinary Barracks is not the only haunted area at Fort Leavenworth.

Sounds of tea parties are still heard in the empty parlor of the Chief of Staff's quarters.

In 1875, the original St. Ignatius Chapel church and rectory burned down, claiming the life of Father Fred, a young priest who had been assigned there. After the fire, the salvageable building material was used to build a house. Some of the scorched bricks were used in and can still be seen making up the fireplace in the dining room. Several names are etched into these bricks, including that of Father Fred. Many who have lived there have claimed to see Father Fred, dressed in his cassock, walking through the house, up and down the stairs, in the kitchen and in the dining room. In the 1970s his robed figure even appeared in a Polaroid photograph taken at a dinner party. After the first chapel burned down, a new one was built on a different site. In the early morning hours of December 16, 2000, it too was completely destroyed by fire.

General George Armstrong Custer has been seen roaming the first floor of The General's Residence where he was court-marshaled at a hearing held in 1867. Accused of leaving his command and mistreating his troops, he was found guilty and given a year's suspension without pay.

The Officers' Quarters is also said to host a previous resident. The apparition of a man with a mustache and goatee once appeared in the fireplace in the middle of a burning fire. When the fired died, the face lingered at the back of the fireplace. This same man has also been seen in one of the bedrooms and in the bathroom with an old-fashioned razor and shaving cream. Loud footsteps up and down the stairs, doors slamming, scratching noises, and loud crashes have been heard throughout the house and some residents have reported icy cold spots in various parts of the house.

The oldest house on base, The Rookery was built in 1832 and has been occupied continually since then. It is said to be haunted by several ghosts who have given the house the reputation of being the most haunted house in the State of Kansas. Seen most often is a woman with long hair who rushes at people with her fingers clawing in attack. No one knows who she is but the legend is that she was a victim of violence. Often noticed is an elderly woman seen chattering in a corner. A young girl is also often seen throwing a tantrum. And, as residents settle for the night, they often report being rousted by a bushy haired old man in a nightshirt

General and Mrs. Philip H. Sheridan occupied the Sheridan House in 1869. General Sheridan left his wife on her deathbed to travel to Chicago on business. She died before his return and is said to haunt the Sheridan House.

Numbers 16 and 18 Sumner Place are a duplex. A kind woman in a black woolen dress and shawl haunted number 16. Legend says she was the nanny/housekeeper who lived in the attic. She seemed to look after the families that lived there by trying to help with domestic chores. She also looked after the children, trying to calm them when they were upset. One child told his parents that a nice lady would read stories to him at night before he went to sleep. One time, a book was found that didn't belong to the family living there. This kindly lady does not, it seems, like babysitters or grandmothers who have reported being firmly pushed out of a child's room.

One family in number 16 was so uncomfortable having her in the house with them that an exorcism was conducted. The lady in black left number 16 and moved into number 18, and continues to take care of that house and its children. She has been seen looking out of the attic window.

In 1880, Catherine and Hiram Sutter stopped at Fort Leavenworth on their way to the Oregon Territory. Catherine sent her two children out to collect firewood and they never came back. After three days, the search party gave the children up for dead but the Sutters stayed on still hoping to find their children, Ethan and Mary. Catherine spent many hours day and night, walking through the snow calling out to them, searching for them. She contracted pneumonia as a result of this and died that winter; she is buried in the cemetery at Fort Leavenworth.

In the Spring of 1881, Hiram Sutter returned to his home in Indiana. Not long after, he received a message that his children were alive and well. They had fallen into the river and were rescued by a group of Fox Indians who took care of them until Spring and returned them to the Fort. Catherine, however doesn't seem to know her children are safe and she continues to walk the Fort searching for them. Wearing a calico dress and black shawl, she is seen carrying a lantern as she searches and sometimes is only heard calling in the darkness.

People have reported seeing Chief Joseph of the Nez

Perce, who was held at Fort Leavenworth in 1877 and, of course, Civil War soldiers have been seen walking through the nearby woods.

Apparently a number of people have never realized they were discharged. The Old Disciplinary Barracks can be found at Fort Leavenworth, Kansas 66027.

FFI: www.legendsofamerica.com/OZ-Forts.html and www.forgottenoh.com/Encounters/leavenworth.html.

Carol MacDonald Menchu, a native of Montana, is a self-described impressionist poet. She is the editor of the *Gabriel Writer*, the monthly newsletter for San Gabriel Writers' League in Georgetown, Texas. She also does some freelance special interest writing for the local newspaper, edits two other newsletters, makes birthday cards for her eight grandchildren, puzzle books, and other graphic art work when her "Muse is out to pasture." Carol has lived in Texas since 1972 where she shares five acres with assorted deer, raccoons, possums, two indoor cats and whoever else wanders by.

Photo by Dawn Bowers, PR Director, Fort Wayne, IN Ghost Trackers

Halloween, Anytime You Want It - 1875

Columbia City Jail, Columbia City, IN

by Jennifer Zamaites

My first encounter at the Columbia City Jail occurred in the cell area on the main floor. Our investigative team was waiting quietly, hoping to observe any abnormal occurrences. I chose to take a seat in the second-to-last cell on the block, just to rest for a moment. In the darkness, I suddenly felt a hand grasp my right leg and slowly move up until it reached my knee.

"Light, light, I need light! Now!" I shouted.

My partner shined his flashlight in the cell and found nothing visible. Despite our searching, we could find nothing, not even critters for that matter, which may have caused it. The local legends I had heard so much about seemed to be true.

The Columbia City Jail, built in 1875, has played an integral part in the history of the town. Located about 30 minutes outside of Fort Wayne, Indiana in Whitley County, it was witness to many of the hardships settlers had to endure. Because of this, the jail has had many uses. It has been a courthouse, jail, and a private residence. Even as a commercial haunted house, open during the Halloween season, as it is used now, its history seems to emanate from its brick exterior. Those who walk by often give it a second glance as if unsure there is no one there in this supposedly resident-free building.

As paranormal investigators with the Indiana Ghost Trackers, we focus on the scientific side of hauntings. Hoping to obtain evidence of the existence of ghosts, we utilize various pieces of equipment, such as IR (infra-red) thermometers, electromagnetic field meters, Geiger counters, digital and 35mm cameras, voice and video recorders, to name just a few. Usually, the first indication that something unusual is going on is your equipment's reaction to a location.

When it comes to the Columbia City Haunted Jail, it never fails that all will be working properly, yet when you get on site, fresh batteries are now dead, cameras begin to malfunction, and hand-held radios find nothing but interference. While often this can be explained by the power structure of the area, it forces you to pay a little closer attention. As a test to find the reason for the strange equipment behavior, we killed the power in the building completely and still the same thing happened. Investigators must also listen to what their bodies are picking up at a location. At this jail, when you walk in the front doors, you can physically feel the air change to an atmosphere alive with electricity. If you are lucky enough to have your equipment working, commonly, your electromagnetic field meter will go off and then cease abruptly, as if an energy source just passed.

On one occasion, two other investigators and I were taking

a break from the investigation in the costume room on the second floor. While all were relaxing, we saw a chain mail costume begin move on its own. All at once, we heard from the corner of the room, rustling of props and a man's voice. The voice, while sounding very real, was just distant enough to be unintelligible.

We shared our experiences with Paul Harrington, the proprietor, who operates the jail as a commercial haunted house. He told us we must have run into Charles Butler, the jail's most famous ghost.

As a young man, Charles Butler had murdered his wife Abbie in 1883. The police promptly apprehended and jailed him, but Butler, along with four other inmates, escaped from the jail. Paul explained that the corner, from which we heard the disembodied voice, was the location where Butler and the others had pried apart the stone ceiling of their cell to gain access to the upper floor. From there, the inmates proceeded to climb out onto the roof. After fashioning a rope of bed sheets, they made their escape during a time when the sheriff had left the inmates alone to visit family in another town.

Upon returning, the sheriff was greeted by the sight of bed sheets blowing in the wind and an empty jail. Butler was later recaptured and, on October 10th, 1884, was taken to the jail's courtyard to be executed by hanging. Unfortunately, Butler did not die immediately due to an imperfect drop and was carried back inside where he later passed away in one of the front rooms. The intensity of Butler's passing was well known and Frank Allwein, the sheriff and executioner felt its effects. He was quoted as saying. "We all have experiences in our lives that we can't forget. The only hanging in Whitley County is something I could never blot from my mind."

The uppermost floor has also proven to be quite active. Workers have reported that despite their best efforts to close it, the door at the top of the stairs always ends up open. It has also been reported that when the jail was used as the sheriff's residence, he witnessed an apparition coming down the stairs toward him.

Needless to say, this seemed a logical place to set up for our next investigation. After about twenty minutes, a tricycle, which is a prop from the haunted house, moved its way across the room as if being pushed or ridden by an unseen visitor. All agreed that they had thoroughly checked for a logical explanation and, to this day, none has been found.

I find that the spirits of the jail seem to become more active when you just sit, talk, laugh than when you search them out. On an overnight investigation, six of us were taking a break in one of the front rooms at around 3 AM. Suddenly, an overwhelming sense of being watched came over us. Next, we clearly heard someone walking around the cell area.

Knowing that we were locked in to prevent any trespassers, I figured someone had broken in, thinking no one was there. Another IGT member and I immediately went to get rid of what we thought were thrill-seeking teenagers, but were unable to find anyone. The entire team split up and searched the building, only to find the doors were all still locked and we were indeed alone. Throughout the next three hours we heard a man laughing, footsteps running, and something knocking. The feeling of being watched would come and go. Curtains that separated some of the rooms would suddenly move as if someone had passed through them, yet no explanation was found.

We have continued to investigate this fascinating location and have been able to obtain much evidence of paranormal activity. If you ever get a chance to visit the jail during the Halloween season, you may want to keep in mind that not only do the living take enjoyment in scaring you. The dead seem to enjoy it, too.

The jail is located at the corner of Washington & Market Streets in downtown Columbia City.

Jennifer Zamaites is the Northeast Regional Director of the non-profit organization, Indiana Ghost Trackers. Raised in Massachusetts and now calling home Fort Wayne, Indiana, Jennifer has always been interested in the paranormal. Growing up in a haunted house left her searching for answers and more importantly proof of life after death. In 2002, she finally found a safe haven for her interests and joined the Fort Wayne Chapter of Indiana Ghost Trackers. IGT provides private investigations and education for the public and its members at no cost. The sincere desire for answers and professionalism won her over, and now she finds herself conducting private investigations as well as ghost hunts for members more interested in a less restrictive atmosphere. Anyone who is on the same quest for answers is encouraged to visit their main website: www.indianaghosts.org.

Photo by Stacey Hasbrook

Ghost Hunt At Buffalo Gap - 1879

First Taylor County Courthouse-Jail, Buffalo Gap, TX

by Joan Upton Hall

You can't blame the ghosts at Buffalo Gap Historic Village for not knowing it's the 21st century. The compound, which occupies a block in the middle of town, is comprised of almost 20 vintage buildings, each one fully furnished according to its appropriate era, and represents the last 50 years of the Old West. As you meander along the trails among chickens, cats, and old fashioned gardens, you might expect the original inhabitants to show up at any minute. In fact, countless visitors and staff swear that at least some of them do. These spirits must wonder why we visitors dress so unfashionably.

As editor of this book, I felt the need for an exact understanding of the procedures ghost investigators use. Not far from where I live, I found Central Texas Ghost Search (CTGS) and was impressed by what I read about them. I contacted Sarah Zell, president of the group, and told her about the book project. When she offered me a chance to experience an actual ghost investigation and asked where I'd like to go, I immediately thought of Buffalo Gap Historic Village. I had visited it before for historical research, and I remembered tales of hauntings in and around the fine old, two-story stone Courthouse-Jail. Sarah liked the idea and made the arrangements.

Sad to say, the town held its county seat status only from 1878-1883, with this original Taylor County Courthouse-Jail constructed in 1879. Blessed with tall trees and abundant ground water, Buffalo Gap occupies a point in the Callahan Divide that cuts through to the flat lands—an oasis before the plains. For hundreds of years, buffalo had beaten a trail followed later by cattle drives. Why would such a place be virtually abandoned? The railroad bypassed it. When tracks were laid east to west through the new town of Abilene a few miles to the north, many residents pulled up stakes and moved there. And soon the county seat went with them.

People lived in the Courthouse-Jail for some time. Then thanks to historians Ernest Wilson and Dr. R. Lee Rhode who owned it at different times beginning in 1956, not only that building was saved as a museum, but other buildings were brought in as well. The only one older than the Courthouse is an 1875 tiny log cabin, moved in from six miles away. Formerly it had been home to a buffalo hunter and his family. In 1999 the Grady McWhiney Research Foundation, affiliated with McMurry University, bought the Village to be further developed and operated as an educational facility. Now enclosed inside a fence, Texas history is not only saved, but shared with all who come to visit, and the staff provides not only static displays but special events with living history interpretations as well.

Among the other seasonal events that bring in crowds, the Village staff goes all out on—bet you can guess—a Halloween tour. Justin Frazier, Site Manager, says one of the scary surprises they set up was a dummy of a man hanging by the neck. Justin got his own surprise when kids asked, "But who's the lady with him?"

Kids also ask from time to time, "Who's the guy in the jail cell?" That cell, once reserved for "hostile" prisoners, stays locked, and in the case of both the tree and cell, Justin says there's nobody there.

Personally, I'm not so sure. Before the hunt, writer/photographer Stacey Hasbrook and I went to look over the place during daylight hours and get photos about closing time. On the second floor of the Courthouse-Jail, a large room that used to serve as the "run about" for ordinary prisoners now houses a collection of guns and Indian artifacts. The single corner cell is at the head of the stairs.

Plastered stone makes up three sides, and its boilerplate steel wall has a barred door with a padlock. A single high, narrow window allows scant daylight and ventilation. Justin unlocked the door for me, but as soon as I entered the gloomy cell with its uninviting cot and a straight chair, I wanted out. I'd like to say the oppressive sensation came from the afternoon heat and semi-darkness, but prickles up and down my spine and my bristling neck hair told me otherwise.

In the interests of journalism, I checked it out thoroughly, but in record time. Feeling anything but alone, I was convinced the "hostile cell" was a fitting place for my invisible companion. Later that evening, during CTGS's search, both the psychics, Tracey Cordero and her daughter Lisa also felt a presence, as did Stacey.

The Courthouse-Jail had been built to serve the county forever. Rows of cannon balls were sandwiched between the large stone blocks in spaces hollowed out for them. This not only held the walls straight, but also thwarted the efforts of any prisoner who tried to escape by scraping out the mortar to loosen the stones. The ground floor contained offices for the County Clerk, the Judge, and the Sheriff as well as a courtroom.

For those few short years, prisoners from "the wild town of Abilene" were brought here, but no one seems to know what incorrigibles might have been locked in the cell that gave us the creeps. After the county seat was moved, and this jail was no longer needed, a family lived on the second floor for a time. What must it have been like to walk past that cell every time you went up or downstairs?

Nowadays, throughout the Village, recorded sounds add to the mood such as a Victrola playing music in the parlor of the marshal's house and distant sounds of trains at the railroad depot. Justin says people compliment the staff on these details, plus other sounds he can't account for. At the marshal's house, it's table conversation. At the schoolhouse, it's the sound of footsteps as of a teacher walking up and down the rows and, at least once, a visitor captured children's voices on tape.

Plenty of the activity occurs in Marshal John Tomas Hill's house, a charming little white cottage only a few feet from the Courthouse-Jail. Like most of the other buildings in the compound, this one was moved to the site. This home of Abilene's first marshal was built in 1881, the same year Abilene was founded. Hill had been shot in the toe during an altercation and, although the infected toe was later amputated, he died of complications. His wife and spinster daughter lived out their lives and also died in that house. It is known that, as was the custom at the time, at least the marshal's funeral, if not all three, took place at home.

The summer of 2002 when I first visited the Village, I had interviewed some McMurry University students working there, part of McWhiney Foundation's history intern program. The young men told me they weren't fond of going into Marshal Hill's house although they all assured me they never used to believe "any of that stuff about ghosts." Josh White, who had worked there for two years, opened up and told of a day he was dusting the artifacts in the Hill house. A feeling of being watched made him turn around. And there he saw a lady in an old fashioned dress walking down the hall.

Tyler Barnett said he shared the same feelings about the place and added that they find little things moved from place to place. He also recalled another incident involving a friend of theirs, who wasn't on hand for the interview. The young intern had been weeding along the edge of the house when he looked up. The lady stood at the window watching him.

Thomas Onger had only been on the job for three days. Until he asked questions about his own eerie feelings, the others hadn't told him about it.

The haunting has evidently been going on for a long time. Josh said one man who came by explained he had visited the Village at least ten years earlier when he was a kid with a school group. Inside the Marshal's house, he had stopped to look through an old photograph album. When a shadow caught his attention, he turned and saw the lady. Shaken, he ran outside, but then brought his buddies back in with him. The album was gone.

The visitor's story made Josh curious, so he and the other guys looked all through the house for an old photograph album, but such a book was nowhere to be found. The next day when Josh went in, the book was lying on the bed. He looked through it and replaced it, but the next time he returned, the album was gone again.

But let's get back to my first-ever ghost hunt in 2005. We met at 10 PM and finished at about 2 AM. Sarah Zell's CTGS team conducted an orderly and thorough investigation in each building reputed to be active. Justin had opened the barriers that are usually in place inside the buildings to keep visitors from handling items on display.

As we began, Sarah explained the procedure. To record possible EVPs (Electronic Voice Phenomenon), everyone sat absolutely quiet while several team members ran audio tapes. One leader would announce our presence, invite any spirits present to communicate, and ask for a name and year. If anyone in the group coughed or there was an outside sound such as a cat fight, barking dogs, or a car driving by, the leader would acknowledge it so there would be no question later when listening.

To collect other data, team members walked around, some with IR (infra-red non-contact) temperature gauge, some with EMF (electronic magnetic field) monitors, several with cameras, and some of us simply with open minds. Sarah told us novices that anyone taking a photo was to announce "Flash" so that no one else would shoot at the same time. This prevented misleading flashes of light from showing up later. The shots were taken in any area where unseen activity was likely. Someone monitored the temperature at all times.

Several orbs did appear from different cameras, but the most interesting anomaly appeared as a frowning face coming out of a wall that had looked to all of us like a plain paneled wall. Paulina Murnahan, who took the shot, was as surprised as the rest of us (shown at the end of the book).

One event took place in the courtroom while we were all being quiet, and the taping was going on as the leader invited the spirits to communicate. I saw two team members react simultaneously to what they both afterward called a "growl," yet this didn't show up on any of the tapes.

Other unexplainable sounds did show up later on the tapes, sounds that none of us had heard, sounds that only came out on one tape each. In answer to one of the questions, there was a loud, metallic sounding screech. The other sound was a muffled male voice that sounded like, "Help me!"

In Marshal Hill's house, psychic Tracey reported a very

bad feeling in one certain spot of the parlor, a feeling she described as "grief, intense sadness, like a funeral." After we all went outside, I asked her if she knew the Marshal's funeral had taken place in the house. Startled, she answered that she never reads the literature ahead of time as she wants to keep an open mind to whatever comes up. Justin confirmed that the funeral almost certainly took place in the parlor.

Could the ethereal lady that folks see be the Marshal's wife or daughter?

Some of the strangest events took place in the Village's two-room school. While the school has no relation to the jail, I include this episode to explain some of the more unusual aspects of this ghost investigation.

The psychics, Tracey and her daughter Lisa, had visited this site a couple of months earlier. Although Lisa had never before done automatic writing (writing down freely whatever comes to her from outside her own mind), she picked up a piece of chalk and wrote on the board a girl's first and last name, but perhaps because of their own surprise at the name coming out of nowhere, they didn't pursue it further. Out of respect for the feelings of surviving family members, I won't include the deceased child's name here, but will call her "Mary."

We all went in and sat at the small, old-fashioned desks on each of which was a slate and chalk. The room was well lighted, and we talked for a few minutes before Lisa picked up a slate. At first she just drew spirals in a leisurely manner, but gradually she picked up speed and began to scribble words as she spoke aloud to "Mary" and wrote answers on the slates that we all kept supplying her with.

One guy blurted out, "Ask her about Steve," though later he said he had no idea where the idea came from. The automatic writing went on sometimes furiously while Lisa's hand obviously began to cramp. It was a sad tale, sketchy at best, but the gist of it was that "Mary" was staying around in an effort to protect her little brother, Steve, who "Daddy hurt," and she wanted Lisa to help her.

While this was going on, Sarah was sitting with her recorder in her hands, its cord dangling. Quietly, she said, "Something keeps tugging at my cord. I thought it was the cat, but he's not here." She said it went on for three or four minutes.

Then Morgan Pipkin, sitting beside her, said, "Ow!" and grabbed his side a couple of times. He said something jabbed him.

The thermometer reading in the room was about 90°, but when the monitor was held near Sarah and Morgan, the reading suddenly dropped about ten degrees.

Over all, I would say there's little question that the collection of historical buildings at Buffalo Gap harbors a few restless spirits. Before the hunt, people who had gotten wind of it wanted to watch, but a crowd would not be conducive to spirit activity. Because of public interest, however, Justin Frazier, as Site Manager, asked Sarah Zell if she would be willing to teach a class on the basics of ghost investigation at the Village periodically, and she agreed.

The town of Buffalo Gap is about eight miles south of Abilene on Highway 89, otherwise known as Buffalo Gap Road. Buffalo Gap Historic Village is located at the corner of Elm and William Street. FFI about the educational programs: (325) 572-5211 www.buffalogap.com or
www.mcwhiney.org/buffalogap.html.

The author's special appreciation goes to Site Manager, Justin Frazier, who went beyond the call of duty in answering questions and serving as a guide. Also especially to Sarah Zell, who teaches science at Cisco Junior College in Abilene. Sarah is president and founder of the Central Texas Ghost Search organization, who put the event together and gave me a firsthand understanding of how ghost investigation works.

People in the area can register for the above mentioned classes online at the CTGS website: www.centraltexasghostsearch.com

Photo by Don Hall

Joan Upton Hall taught English for 28 years while she and her husband raised three children. During that time she was editor and cartoonist of a national-award-winning teacher newsletter. Now a full-time author/ editor, Joan wrote *Rx for Your Writing Ills* (1998; 2nd ed. 2003), that has helped hundreds of struggling writers. A frequent speaker at writers' conferences, she continues to teach writing workshops. Besides publishing numerous short stories and articles, she also contributes a self-syndicated column for various writers' newsletters as well as travel and humor columns for the county newspaper.

In 2002 she published *Grand Old Texas Theaters That Won't Quit* (Republic of Texas Press), co-authored with Stacey Hasbrook. Joan was researching a similar book about historical state jails when Atriad Press offered her a chance to edit this anthology, *Ghostly Tales from America's Jails*. Previous to that, she had contributed a story about a pet haunting in one of Atriad's *Haunted Encounters* series.

Her largest project to date is her fantasy trilogy, *Excalibur Regained* (Zumaya Publications), which combines Arthurian legend, reincarnation, and bio-terrorism set in a near-future world. The first novel, *Arturo el Rey*, debuted in 2005, and sequels will come out annually. For updates, visit: www.JoanUptonHall.com.

Photo courtesy on Folsom Historical Society

Dead Men Walking - 1880

Folsom Prison, Represa, CA

by Olyve Hallmark Abbott

California's Folsom Prison is "Motel 6,000" for that many inmates—plus ghosts. Throughout this penitentiary's history, apparitions are reputed to have served an extended sentence. A substantial number of inmates and corrections officers believe Folsom to be haunted. Officers know unexplained activities have been reported for decades. A few believe the reports to be false; still others offer no comment. Who can tell for sure unless he is a witness?

In 1878, authorities chose an area with unlimited native stone on which to erect Folsom Prison. The American River provided a natural boundary for the complex. In the beginning, the prison had 50 cells for 100 prisoners, and San Quentin transferred the first ones there. Animosity transferred with them.

Plans to complete Folsom had been hurried up so that prison labor could be used to build a dam, and the prison was completed in 1880. Convicts worked the quarries, providing material for a granite wall. They observed no safety precautions, and prisoners as well as a guard were killed in quarry accidents.

Even before the wall's completion, the prison experienced many escape attempts. On one occasion three convicts used a hijacked prison train to smash through the gate. Guards recaptured two of them. Who knows where the third escaped? Chances are good that he never returned as a ghost.

Desperation motivated many other attempts through the years. For example, one inmate showed ingenuity in constructing a diving suit from a football bladder, goggles, lenses, and a few other useful items he had scavenged. He planned to swim underwater across the powerhouse millpond. According to a former officer who now volunteers in the prison museum, the escapee made the breathing tube too short. This drowned inmate may very well be one of Folsom's ghost squad.

What situation would make men so desperate?

Convicts who wore horizontal black and white striped uniforms were at the bottom of the heap. They had no privileges whatsoever. Those wearing vertical stripes had slightly more privileges and had the right of overseeing small groups of the horizontally clad inmates. They all wore black-brimmed hats.

In the early days, privileged or not, convicts ate from tin plates nailed to the tables. After a meal, a crew would dump water on the plates, brush them off with a short broom, and the plates would be ready for the next meal. So much for sanitary conditions.

Until electricity became available in 1893, candles and oil

lamps provided the only light as well as heat for the cells. Doors of solid iron rather than bars allowed little or no light. The doors had six-inch slots through which to see. Not until the 1940s did the prison drill air holes about the size of half-dollars in the doors.

To settle disturbances, guards hanged rabblerousing prisoners by the thumbs or hobbled them with ankle weights. For psychological effect, to keep inmates from thinking discipline was lax, on the first of each month, guards fired gatling guns from six towers.

Bill Lindelof interviewed Folsom Prison Lieutenant Tom Ayers for an article in the *Sacramento Bee* (Feb. 28, 2001). Asked about working the graveyard shift, the prime time for ghostly occurrences, the lieutenant said, "We are 121 years old. We have a very violent history. A lot of men died here."

If science cannot explain a phenomenon, it's quite possibly a true supernatural occurrence. Lieutenant Ayers admitted that in certain places around midnight, "the hair would stand up on the back of your neck." On other occasions, a presence is unmistakably nearby. You can't hear or see anything. You just know someone's there. Lieutenant Ayers is not only a historian but also a prison spokesman. He has often been a host for the Folsom Prison tours. Inasmuch as their museum has many artifacts and photographs concerning its bloody and colorful history, it offers tours to give a better idea of prison life of the past—and present.

The third floor of the medical clinic once housed the insane. Apparitions are said to walk through these halls. It seems ghosts of former inmates have the entire prison at their disposal. Some of the rooms have been so invaded by spirits the Catholic Church interceded. The chaplain of the prison prayed to God that everything evil be cast out. A prisonsorcism?

A dungeon of cells on the first floor of Guard Tower 13 once held obstinate prisoners. Correctional officers on the third floor have reported sounds of creaking cell doors from the dungeon below. Of course, a spirit could walk through the bars, but the ghost of a previous inmate might open and close the door just to show he can, when it had been impossible in life.

One exhibit in the museum shows thick hemp ropes used to execute inmates by hanging before the state ceased that method of execution. Each condemned man had his own personal rope, later tagged with the man's inmate number. After the execution, officials moved the corpse to the morgue and sounded a large bell 13 times. Out of tradition, they still ring the bell at five o'clock each day. Do the ghosts know for whom the bell tolls?

Perhaps one of the eeriest tales concerns Folsom's oldest cellblock, Building 5, the site of the gallows. If it isn't too dark, observers can see four silent apparitions in the shadows of the stone building. They don't do anything but gather there. Some people claim to be able to see the eyes of specters.

It is said that a "laundry man" inmate walks the age-old Cellblock #5. He isn't going to the laundry but turns into the same cell every time. The laundry man doesn't deliver clean clothes. He vanishes from the spot. Time and tide wait for no ghost.

Death Row in Folsom Prison held 93 men through the years, waiting for their just or unjust rewards. One wonders how many men were condemned to death for crimes they did not commit. If they were unjustly hanged, do their spirits return to haunt those who confined them? Or do they sleep in deserved eternal peace?

Customarily, the hangman of Folsom Prison received the day off after completing an execution. He also received ten dollars and a bottle of booze. The first of 93 men was hanged at Folsom in December of 1895 and the last in 1937. At that time, California changed from executions by hanging in Folsom to a gas chamber in San Quentin.

"Old Death Row" held 13 cells. When an inmate arrived in

cell #13, the one closest to the gallows, the guards recorded his weight and neck measurements. They pre-stretched the rope to lessen the bounce—a jolting visual. When a prisoner's final hour ended, the next prisoner in line would move into the just-vacated cell, one space closer to the gallows. You can still see the metal ring on the ceiling that held the noose.

Since these inmates were not allowed to talk to each other from one cell to the next, they whispered just loud enough so the guards could not hear. Whispering can still be heard on Death Row.

Whispering also takes place in the old prison morgue where inmates' bodies were stored before burial. With so much violence, bloodshed, and murders taking place in Folsom, it's no wonder ghosts spend time wandering freely about. Experts say when death is violent, the victim's spirit—shall we say—hangs around.

The operating room, located on the clinic's third floor, provides an atmosphere of chilled apprehension. Sometimes convicts died on the operating table, and those long dead inmates still make audible disturbances at night.

In 1927, a prison riot broke out. The melee ended with the death of an officer. On misty mornings, his spirit, the "Folsom Phantom," patrols the top of the prison walls. If an inmate's ghost ever confronted the officer's ghost, what would their reactions be?

The prison staff doesn't volunteer much about supernatural tales of Folsom, but they will gladly answer visitors' questions on the subject. Both believers and skeptics are eager to hear about paranormal activity. Lieutenant Ayers said his own experience concerning an anomaly occurred on the graveyard shift. He saw "someone in a suit and wearing a hat" walk down a corridor. When he investigated, he found no one. After all, a ghost can disappear in and out of cells whenever the spirit moves him.

Hauntings aside, Folsom's notoriety has spread from such

movies as *The Jericho Mile* starring Peter Strauss, *Riot in Cellblock 11* starring Neville Brand, and *American Me* starring Edward James Olmos. It was furthered in song with, "Time Keeps Draggin' On," as Johnny Cash sang in "Folsom Prison Blues." It's true, Johnny spent time at the prison—to sing for the inmates in 1968.

For 114 years, Folsom served as a maximum-security unit, housing incorrigibles and the condemned. Real life inmates included "Little Pete" Fong Ching, Mafia kingpin in the 1880s; Charles Manson (from 1972-1976); Eric Menendez; and Rick James. The prison switched to medium-security in the mid-1990s and now has a minimum unit. Parts of the prison have been converted into a museum. Tower 13, a peaked gothic structure, offers an intimidating view of Folsom State Prison, not your typical vacation spot. Visitors take pictures of a place they like to visit, but they wouldn't want to live there. For information about visiting, contact: Folsom Prison, 300 Prison Road, P.O. Box 71, Represa, CA 95671. Phone: (916) 985-2561

Photo by Taryn Wilson

Olyve Hallmark Abbott first became interested in the paranormal when she wrote *Ghosts in the Graveyard: Texas Cemetery Tales.* Since that time, she has been invited by paranormalists to accompany them on investigations where she had a couple of eerie experiences of her own. She is a speaker for various groups in the state, including schools, libraries, women's clubs, and heraldry organizations. Olyve's stories are in the first two books of the Atriad Press *Haunted Encounters* series. Her *Lone Star Ghosts* placed first in the Oklahoma Writers' Federation Competition's nonfiction book category.

She is editor of Hawkins Heritage, a genealogical quarterly. At present, Olyve is finishing her first novel, *TV-Live—Or Dead*, a murder mystery with paranormal overtones.

She turned to writing after a musical career in opera, musical comedy, and network television, having worked with Beverly Sills, Carl Reiner, and Sid Caesar. A graduate of SMU, she also attended Juilliard School of Music and studied opera with Dame Eva Turner of the Royal Academy in London.

Olyve lives in Fort Worth, and has two daughters: Taryn Wilson and Devon Mihesuah.

Photo by Don Hall

The Ghost Who Likes Me - 1881

Bandera County Jail - Bandera, TX

by Stephanie Parker Logue

It takes a measure of courage to work at a small town newspaper—especially if the assignment involves investigating a ghost of historic proportions. Judith Pannebaker and I, both staff writers at The *Bandera Review* newspaper at the time, spent Halloween night 2003 in Bandera's Old Jail building to meet resident ghost "Harvey."

The two-story limestone block building, constructed in 1881 as Bandera County's second jail was designed by English architect Alfred Giles. At the time, it was named the "best built jail in the state." Iron cages were installed on the top floor for prisoner cells, though the cells have been gone since 1942 when the scrap iron was given to the war effort. The jailer's room was located on the first floor. Specifications called for a metal roof and "water closets" (bathrooms). Huge limestone blocks were hand quarried from the riverbed and carried on livestock-drawn wagons.

Bandera's first jail, located on Main Street, had been only a 14x14-foot room, constructed of 6x6 cypress timbers, with only one small window near the top. There was no door, only an opening on top of the building. A ladder was used to enter and exit the jail. After they climbed down inside the building, prisoners were chained to a ring in the floor, and then the ladder was pulled back up. Unlike the "secure" 1881 rock jail, no prisoner ever escaped that first jail.

The 1881 building now serves as an office for the water district. Water district employees are proud of Harvey, and welcomed us reporters in. They say he is harmless and does not scare people. Perhaps Harvey doesn't scare them, but two separate cleaning crews now refuse to clean the building at night and have changed their schedules to allow them to clean the old jail during daylight hours. Because Judith and I wanted to be objective, we refrained from interviewing the cleaning crews until after we had spent the night at the old jail. Still, we had heard about Harvey's "tricks."

Harvey had been credited with turning lights on in the front of the building while someone was in the back room. He had reportedly flicked lights off and on, creaking across the floor with the measured tread of footsteps. He had rolled chairs out from under desks at night while the building was empty and surfed the Internet at approximately 3 a.m. The number three, we discovered, is important to Harvey.

Not believing in ghosts—even Harvey—the water district manager set up a video camera over the front door of the old jail one weekend. He wanted to find out what employee was entering the building off-hours and playing tricks that were perhaps maliciously intended to frighten other employees. The motion-activated video camera turned on at exactly 3:30 a.m.

and 3:30 p.m. the entire weekend, but nothing was displayed on film.

Those who work with Harvey in the office on a daily basis claim that his most distinctive activity is the "plinking" noise he makes. The noise seems to come from the conference room, which at one time housed jail cells and prisoners.

The janitorial crew claims that Harvey's most distinctive activity is—everything! "I don't believe in ghosts, but I don't clean at night anymore," is the usual response to Harvey-related questions.

Both those who work in the building and those who clean it attribute a loud "whack!" to Harvey. They explain that the noise is like the sound a box would make if it were dropped from the ceiling. Both say that the front doorbell has rung when no one has entered or left the building. The back room, where the restrooms are located, has been described as "a creepy place where the pressure seems to change."

I must admit that real or not, Harvey has a sense of humor. He seems to like me.

As a newswoman, I attend water board meetings in the jail, with its huge limestone-block walls, high tin ceiling and bar-encased windows with peeling paint dripping off the sagging wooden trim. Some parts of the ceiling are painted blue, a trick used by old-timers to trick wasps into thinking the ceiling was sky so they wouldn't build nests there.

During meetings, I sit on a hard wooden bench where I can study the rock-slab floor where long-ago prisoners chipped their names and pictures into stone with eating utensils. One prisoner, described as "insane," dug the masonry cement out from around a huge limestone block with his spoon, pushed the block out and nearly made his escape before he was discovered. My gaze travels around the huge stones that were so skillfully fitted together into a pattern that married large and small limestone rocks into a union that has survived 124 years of use and several careers. When I leave the jail after the meeting is over, I feel as if I am leaving a friend behind. Leaving—that's the problem because of Harvey's sense of humor.

Out of all the people who use the jail during the day and attend the water district meetings at night, I seem to be the only one who gets locked in the women's bathroom! I'm so afraid of interrupting the meeting or embarrassing myself by pounding on the door and yelling for help that I've started leaving the door unlocked.

But back to that Halloween night in 2003. Judith and I wanted to know: Is Harvey real? And if he is real, who is he?

When Bandera's new jail and sheriff's office were built behind the courthouse, plans were enacted to tear down the 1881 historic rock building. Citizens heard about the plan in time to stop it. After World War II, veterans ran a welding shop in the cell room, which is now called the conference room. Veterans built a tin shed room in back of the building and studied carpentry. The tin shed now houses county documents, rescued by the Bandera County Historical Commission. Some of the records date back to the mid-1800s.

Names and artwork left behind by former prisoners are forever etched into the cold stone floor that once secured the metal bars of jail cells. It is difficult to match the chipped names, initials and dates to records of jail occupants because the jail was constructed in 1881 and some of the jail records are missing. Crimes that incarcerated Bandera County's wrongdoers between 1881 and 1901 included slander, obstructing a public road, unlawfully leaving gates open, abusive language, adultery, interfering with a religious service, assault and battery, seduction of a young girl, and theft of goats (sentenced to four years in the state prison).

One name, Jack Kelly, repeated itself like an automatic weapon. Kelly was consistently charged with aggravated assault over the years before his name disappeared from jail records. Because he died? In jail perhaps? Could he be

Harvey? Or could Harvey be some other long-ago prisoner who returned to the historic stone building after death released him forever from the cold stone and metal cages?

A local man had escaped from his second-floor prison cell nightly by shinning up the metal bars of his cell and exiting through the high tin ceiling. He would spend the night at home, then check himself back into jail the next morning before his absence could be discovered! Other crimes recorded include charges of "negligently permitting a prisoner to escape"—and murder. Two prisoners held for murder in the old jail were eventually found, "not guilty." Could one of their victims be Harvey? Angry, perhaps, because his killer went unpunished?

Details about prisoners surface again in 1928 under Sheriff Elvious Hicks. Most of the cases were for transporting liquor and driving while intoxicated. While that jail log is not one of the missing ones, entries in it end abruptly. Sheriff Elvious Hicks, 53, was ambushed and killed on March 9, 1932, allegedly by moonshiners. A few minutes after Hicks was shot, Ben Clark was shot three times and killed as he attempted to leave the crime scene. Guns were found in his possession and spent shells were found in his vehicle.

Deputy Billy Burnes was charged with Clark's murder, then acquitted. He was appointed to fill Hicks' unexpired term, and he held the office of sheriff for the next nine successive terms.

So who is Harvey? Judith and I were determined to discover the truth. Both of us had worked a full day, but we settled determinedly at the front desk of the old jail and prepared to stay awake all night. We did hear a few "plinks," but not the steady metallic sound we would have expected had Harvey been carving more pictures into the rock floor. We heard one loud "whop!" as if a box had been dropped from the ceiling to the floor in the conference room that had once held jail cells. We investigated (together) and found nothing.

Unfortunately, we eventually fell asleep, our heads cradled

on our arms on top of the desk. At exactly 3:30 a.m., we both woke up simultaneously. I had seen a dark curtain falling in front of my face while I was asleep. Judith had heard something. We waited until after 4 a.m., and then went home to our own beds to let someone else solve the mystery of Harvey.

Sheriff Elvious Hicks was a known prankster. Once a neighbor complimented him on his son saying, "I've never heard that baby cry." Hicks stayed up until 3 a.m. one night, then took the crying baby to the neighbor's house, explaining after he woke the neighbor up, "I just thought you would want to hear the baby cry."

Hicks was shot three times. His alleged killer was shot three times and died just after midnight, which is 3 p.m. the next day in Australia—which has nothing at all to do with this story except that Harvey—whoever he is or isn't or whether he is or isn't—likes the number three. And, well, there might be a connection.

For some years, the Historical Commission leased the old jail. Today, it is used as office space for the Bandera County River Authority and Groundwater District water district and is located at 202 12th Street in Bandera. No official tours are given, but unless a meeting is in progress, visitors are welcome.

Photo by Gail Joiner

Stephanie Parker Logue is the author of three mystery-romance-suspense books, *Heart Shadows*, *Until the Shadows Flee*, and *Shadow Chase*. The latter two are set in the Texas Hill Country. Logue is a staff writer for the *Bandera County Courier*. Prior to that, she has worked for other newspapers, including the *Lovelock Review-Miner* in Nevada, which is the desert backdrop for Logue's first novel. She has also published fiction and nonfiction in several magazines.

Since her husband of 15 years went home to the Lord in 2004, she lives comfortably with a collie dog and a cat that the dog rescued as a kitten from a flood. This dog has also befriended an opossum that makes nightly forays to the porch of the country house to scarf down seeds scattered from the bird feeder.

Logue has one son, Luke Parker, a U.S. Marine serving in Iraq, and a granddaughter, Dulcinea, not yet two years old and living in North Carolina with her mother, Dr. Delight Thompson-Parker. When Logue is not writing, she is working on a Bible Land theme park near Uvalde, Texas. Her hobbies are rock work and cement creations—which pretty well explain and describe Bible Land.

Photo courtesy of Historical Society of Pottawattamie County

The Squirrel Cage - 1885
Pottawattamie County Jail, Council Bluffs, IA

by Joy Nord

The westward movement across the prairie took a high toll on human life. To have ghosts lingering throughout abandoned forts, battlefields, homes, hotels, and jails should come as no surprise. Today one of the most famous haunted attractions of the northern plains is the "Squirrel Cage," the old historical Pottawattamie County Jail in Council Bluffs, Iowa.

This County became part of the Pottawattamie Purchase of 1847, the name meaning "Blowers of Fire" or "Keepers of the Council Fire" in the language of the Potawatomi tribe who once dwelled within Iowa Territory. Ryan Roenfeld, of the

County's Historical Society, points out that the Potawatomi people don't spell the word the same as the county does.

This Algonquian-speaking people, who originally lived around Lake Michigan, had sold Chicago and most of Illinois, and many moved to western Iowa in 1836-38. There they scattered into several villages, one of which eventually evolved into modern day Council Bluffs, Iowa. Pressured to move farther west in 1846, the Potawatomi exchanged their Iowa reservation for one in Kansas where their descendants still live today near the town of Mayetta.

By 1853, Council Bluffs had become the county seat. The rapidly growing village had more than 7,000 inhabitants, mainly Mormons on their way to Utah from Illinois. It also served as an important supply town for other homesteading pioneers and gold seekers headed for California.

When President Abraham Lincoln indicated Council Bluffs as the eastern terminus for "railway passage" to the West in 1863, he not only set in motion access for adventurous explorers and entrepreneurs, but he also laid the tracks for lawless renegades and war-scarred Civil War veterans looking for a new start.

Like all frontier boomtowns, Council Bluffs had its share of problems. One of which, was how to incarcerate law breakers. After a fire burned the old jail to the ground, a bond election was held for the purpose of building a new courthouse and jail. The bond issue passed and construction began in March 1885.

Although the new structure had the external appearance of a Philadelphia mansion, more than an institution for criminals, its design proved to be a state-of-the-art correctional facility, costing $30,000. Only $8,000 of it went for the exterior paid for a gable roof, large windows, and brown brick walls surrounding the structure. The interior unit cost over $22,000. Why so much more for the inside? Designers, William H. Brown and Benjamin F. Haugh both of Indianapolis, Indiana had stated in their patent issued in July 1881 that, "The object of our invention is to produce a jail in which prisoners can be controlled within the necessity of personal contact between them and the jailer."

This unique, lazy-Susan-style jailhouse was named the "Squirrel Cage" for many years because of its three-story rotary jail cells. Designed to accommodate both male and female prisoners as well as juveniles, the three-story jail was a marvel of engineering and construction. Prisoners were housed in the heart of the facility, which consisted of a drum divided into ten pie-shaped cells on each floor. The drum rotated by a hand-turned crank, therefore lining up only one cell at a time with a single doorway. The front part of the building had offices for the superintendent and jailers, a kitchen, trustee cells, and the women's quarters. Unlike most jails of the time, this one also had indoor toilet facilities.

On September 11, 1885, the Pottawattamie County Jail opened for the transfer of prisoners from the courthouse into the "Squirrel Cage." Fourteen prisoners were moved: twelve men and two women.

Only two prisoners died in the jail during its years in operation, one from a heart attack and the other by an injury he received climbing up to write his name on his cell's ceiling. The ghost experts, however, don't feel that the ghost lingering within the "Squirrel Cage" is a prisoner, but that of the first jailer instead.

The paranormal activity is believed to come from J.M. Carter, who spent more time in the jail than any of his prisoners. After overseeing the jail's construction, he became the first superintendent of it. He and his wife lived in an apartment on the fourth floor, a floor that did not rotate. It is rumored that Carter died in the apartment of a heart attack. Although the jail no longer imprisons the convicted, both staff and prisoners have felt his presence for many years. Complaints about noises and eerie feelings are often made, but no demonic activity seems to occur.

On March 19, 2005, a team from the Paranormal Research & Investigative Studies Midwest (P.R.I.S.M.) visited the jail to take exterior shots of the building. The building remained closed from November 1st to March 31st, so nobody was inside. After examining the pictures on a computer, the team found one particular photo that seemed to capture an image of a man standing by the window on the fourth floor. The team returned on March 20th and 21st to try to recreate the photo, but had no success. However, the P.R.I.S.M. team continues their ongoing investigation.

In 1969 the county closed the "Squirrel Cage" to prisoners. The jail is now part of the National Register of Historic Places, and houses a small museum. Only three of these rotary style jails remain: the one in Council Bluffs, one in Missouri, and one in Indiana. However the Council Bluffs jail was the only three-story "Squirrel Cage" ever built.

This jail is located at 226 Pearl Street, Council Bluffs, Iowa (I-80, Exit 3). The Council Bluffs Historical Society invites you to come and "spend a little time behind bars." FFI: (712) 323-2509, www.thehistoricalsociety.org , and www.doyouseedeadpeople.org.

The following poem gives an idea of how close this unique structure came to demolition:

The Battle of the Squirrel Cage Jail

by
Ida Nelson of Council Bluff

About a hundred years ago in Council Bluffs town
They had a county jail, but it burned down.
So, they built a new Jailhouse and built it very well.
Said, "This fine building should last us for quite a spell."

It was a Mr. Brown's invention—he had features galore,
From pie-shaped cells, to that one narrow, tricky door.
The rotary cellblock was turned by water, or so they say---
No one knows how to this very day.

With thick iron bars and a high steel cage,
This new county Jail was a marvel of the age.
Our Squirrel cage Jailhouse bravely stood without fear,
Holding those villains year after year.

In 1969, Jailhouse's life lay on the line,
Those city Fathers cried, "Tear that Jailhouse down!
We don't want that old building standing 'round!"

Jailhouse heard that awful sound,
Mourned, "don't I have a friend in town?"
The Historical Society listened to its fearful cry.
Their answer was, "We can't let that building be torn down and die.
We looked it over and it isn't all that bad—
Why, it's the most unique building this town ever had."

City Fathers, we beg of you,
We'll take care of this Jailhouse—
We'll be its Jailhouse crew.
It's been here since 1885,
We want that Jailhouse, we want it ALIVE!

Well! There was quite a roar and an awful din.
Through it all I believe that Jailhouse ever managed to smile,
And give a happy grin.
Murmured politely in its new neighbor's ear,
"Didn't really want to be torn down, I like it here!"

Thus, those folks who fought with all their might,

Preserved their Jailhouse and its site.
'Twas 1977 when all those dreams finally came true,
This building now completely owned and protected by its
Faithful Jailhouse crew.

Say, you could almost feel the Jailhouse rock,
And it sang out with glee,
"Those folks bought my building."
You'll see, "I will stand strong and sturdy as can be,
Standing proudly for those friends,
Who stood up for me!"

After dyslexia turned Joy Nord into a non-reader, she only did required reading for many years. When her father passed away in the summer of 2001, her mother suggested reading as a sleep aid. So she picked up a romance novel, and it was "love at first read." Within eighteen months, she had read over 100 books. She decided she could write stories just from her own life experiences—one of which includes "spending a little time behind bars" for a crime she was tricked into committing over 30 years ago.

She is an active member of the Writers' League of Texas, Austin Chapter of Romance Writers of America, and president of the San Gabriel Writers' League in Georgetown, Texas. Joy lives in Round Rock, Texas, with her husband Richard. They have three adult children and four grandchildren. She writes romance novels involving old Western history. Joy invites you to visit her website: www.JoyNord.com.

Photo by Don Hall

Cursed Clock Tower Stops Time - 1887

Gonzales County Jail, Gonzales, TX

by Gary Brown

You can't get the correct time of day in Gonzales, Texas. At least, not from the historic courthouse clock tower. Those four clocks have been out-of-sync or stopped continuously since 1921, the year the last legal hanging was conducted inside the nearby Gonzales County Jail.

The reason the old clocks refuse to work? Legend has it that a condemned inmate sat in his cell staring out his barred window at the courthouse building and watched as the clocks slowly wound down the remaining hours of his life.

During those solitary hours and until the moment the trap door sprang from beneath his feet, he professed his innocence. He was Gonzales County's last executed inmate, but before the hangman's noose ended his time-recording vigil, the man placed a curse upon the clocks that had tormented him so—a curse he claimed would be sustained forever because he was wrongfully executed.

Today, at one location on the second floor, it is possible for visitors to look out through the bars on the windows, through the oak branches and green leaves, and see the clock tower of the courthouse nearby, quite probably the same vantage point as Albert Howard used to count down the hours. And, regardless of the time of day, those clocks will show 4:22.

That cursing ghost is only one of many ghostly legends walking the old Gonzales jail and its surroundings today, but while many of the other spirits may be more famous, none have been as effective in applying a curse.

Gonzales is one of the most historic towns in Texas as well as one of the oldest. The Texas Revolution leading to independence from Mexico started near there and after Colonel William Barret Travis's impassioned plea for reinforcements in the final days of the Alamo siege, 32 Gonzales men responded. They were the only Texans to answer that desperate plea.

Upon news of their deaths, while the smoke of the pyres still hung in the air over the Alamo, Sam Houston ordered the burning of Gonzales to deny Santa Anna the town and its contents. From beneath an oak tree that still stands, Houston gathered the grieving widows of those 32 volunteers, issued his order to burn the town, and began the Runaway Scrape that would end the following month on the plains of San Jacinto with a victory over Santa Anna's army.

The ghosts of the past run deep in Gonzales. During the Republic of Texas period (1836-1845) and the later Mexican War, men from Gonzales participated in nearly every campaign. An earthen fort was built here during the Civil War, and again the local men mustered and marched off to war.

After the Civil War, Reconstruction was a harsh reality in this part of Texas, and Gonzales County found itself, like many other rural areas, inundated with lawless drifters and outlaws.

The outlying lawlessness was so bad that in 1885 the county started construction on a new jail, designed as a "small penitentiary." This was, after all, the period in which Texas feuds were rampant, and jail inmates were often "sprung" from their cells by family or fellow outlaws. On the other hand, this was also the period of the "lynching era" in which many jails were besieged by indignant, (and often drunk) crowds, a cell door torn open, and the inmate hanged from the nearest strong limb.

In 1885 architect Eugene T. Heiner contracted to build this jail that would hold up to 200 prisoners securely in the event of a riot. Heiner subcontracted the actual construction of the building to Henry Kane and the Snead & Company Iron Works. Heiner and Kane designed and constructed a three-story jail of reinforced concrete and metal. Even the ceilings were corrugated steel and concrete. The death cells, probably the most security-sensitive area of any jail, were constructed in a latticework pattern of iron bars two inches wide and a quarter-inch thick that were forged together and fused with heat, borax and rivets.

The jail was completed two years later and was, by any standard, a formidable calaboose and in many ways did resemble a prison. With justification, many argue that the Gonzales County Jail was more secure than the state penitentiary in Huntsville.

It was built like a stone fortress, and the jailer and his family had living quarters on the bottom floor. Also on that floor was the lunatic cell and next to that, the dungeon, or "dark cell." Huge doors sealed this cell and blocked all light. Small holes above the door allowed some air inside. After all, this was south Texas, and no air conditioning was available.

In the center of the jail on the second floor and extending up to the ceiling above the third floor, is an area known as the runabout where the hanging gallows were located. The original was torn down in the 1950's, so the scaffolding today is a reproduction. The second and third floors surrounding this center gallows area consisted of cellblocks, and Heiner's emphasis on security can be seen everywhere. The doors leading to the cellblocks were constructed with swing-out windows that allowed the jailer to inspect the prisoners before the door was unlocked. Inside, the cells could only be opened by use of an isolated and heavily barred box containing a set of levers.

With its opening in 1887, the Gonzales County Jail began almost a century of incarceration that included some of the most colorful and potentially deadly outlaws in Texas history.

Legendary outlaw John Wesley Hardin probably did jail time in Gonzales, but this had to be prior to the construction of the new jail. In 1885-1887 Hardin was serving time in the state penitentiary in Huntsville. In fact, he wouldn't get out of prison until 1894. Passing the state bar exam while in prison, Hardin returned to Gonzales and opened a law office so it is likely he did visit the jail to talk with clients. An original copy of his business card is on exhibit at the jail today.

After the jail was completed, plans were made to build a new courthouse within sight of the barred windows. Hardin may well have seen the beginning construction of the new red brick courthouse nearby but he almost certainly never had the opportunity to consult the clocks in the tower. The courthouse was finished in 1896 and Hardin was long gone from Gonzales—some say "run off." He never returned, leaving a legacy of as many as twenty-five killings. No doubt he also left a ghost or two behind in Gonzales.

Gregorio Cortez was imprisoned here awaiting trial for the murder of a sheriff at the turn of the century. Captured and arrested only after a sensational headline-dominating chase across Texas for the border, Cortez would become a controversial figure in 1901. During that horseback chase across the state, Cortez' wife, his children, his mother, and his sister-in-law were held in the Gonzales County jail without charges as an enticement for Cortez to surrender himself.

He was eventually tried eleven times at various locations before being sentenced to prison for murder. His first trial took place inside the red brick courthouse. He received a fifty-year sentence, and an incensed mob of 300 men tried to break into the jail and lynch him. The jail builders, Heiner and Kane, however, had done their jobs well, and the building proved indeed to be "riot proof." Cortez would eventually be transferred to prison, incarcerated several years, and later pardoned and released. He died shortly after prison discharge, but his run from the Texas Rangers had made him a legend, and his eventual conviction polarized Texans for a generation. Like John Wesley Hardin and the Alamo martyrs, Hispanic folk-hero Cortez also left behind a ghost at Gonzales.

The jail building, which had a "lunatic's cell," would have still been new when Cortez was imprisoned there. When there weren't any lunatics doing time in Gonzales, the cell housed women and even children. This is almost certainly where Gregorio Cortez' wife, children, mother, and sister-in-law stared out through the bars waiting for news of his escape attempt and probably watching the hands of the four clocks on the courthouse tower.

The three death cells look like something from the Spanish Inquisition period. Small boxes, they are constructed entirely of thick iron bars riveted together about two inches apart in a latticework pattern. Inside, a simple bunk and small coal-burning stove were all a condemned man was allowed.

It was here in 1921 that the condemned Albert Howard spent his final days while professing his innocence. From his death cell in the winter months, he probably stoked a fire in his corner stove and otherwise spent his days staring out from his cell through the barred window nearby. About all he could see from that angle was the top of the courthouse where he had been sentenced to die by hanging. As the day grew closer, he must have calculated the number of hours he had left to live.

It has often been said that time stands still for no man, and it did not for Albert Howard. But sometime before his fateful moment on the gallows, he cursed that clock. To prove his innocence after his execution, he predicted, the clock would never again keep time correctly. Albert met his appointment with death on those gallows in the runabout that March 18, 1921 day. Shortly afterward, the clocks began to keep erratic time, each of the four timepieces showing different times or even stopping completely.

Over the years, various efforts were made to repair them but with only temporary successes. As recently 1990, the clocks were repaired and synchronized. But again, the century-old tower began showing false or stopped time. Over a decade after that last repair attempt, the hands of all four clocks were frozen on 4:22.

Was Albert Howard in fact an innocent man unjustly hanged? Nobody knows for sure. The court records indicate that a jury found him guilty. Do the broken clocks on the Gonzales County courthouse verify his claims of innocence? Again, who knows for sure? But Albert Howard, wherever his soul may rest, is probably nodding his head in some degree of satisfaction.

The early community of Gonzales was originally plotted by surveyors in the form of a Spanish cross, consisting of seven town squares. As the community transformed from a Mexican state, to a republic, to an American state and, briefly, a Confederate state, a virtual panorama of history unfolded in or around this old community. Today the seven squares, formed into the shape of a cross, reflect those periods of history and are designated as Texas Heroes Square, Confederate Square, Military Square, Cemetery Square, Church Square and Market Square. At the center of this "cross," is the dominating Courthouse Square that includes the Gonzales County Jail.

The Gonzales County jail, the "riot-proof small prison," did its job well for nearly a century. Closed in 1975, it is now a museum and the headquarters for the local chamber of commerce. There are exhibits, and much of the facility is open to the public on a self-guided basis. The facility is located at 414 St. Lawrence in the historic downtown area of Gonzales. Additional information may be obtained by calling 830-672-6532.

Gary Brown is a historical writer and speaker specializing in military and Texas history. A graduate of the University of Houston and resident of Friendswood, Texas, he has published over seventy articles in regional and national magazines.

His Texas Revolution-era book, *The New Orleans Greys* was a finalist in the New Orleans Public Library literary awards in 1999 and his biography of James Walker Fannin was a finalist for the Presidio La Bahia Award sponsored by the Sons of the Republic of Texas. His collection of Texas prison stories, *Singin' a Lonesome Song*, was selected as the Barnes and Noble Houston-area "Book of the Month" in April 2001. His fourth book, *Texas Gulag*, is a collection of inmate memoirs during the chain-gang years and was featured with an interview on Public Radio in 2002.

He has made presentations to groups including the Daughters of the Republic of Texas, Goliad County Historical Commission, National Society Children of the American Revolution, Texas Historical Commission and various college classes and writer's groups. His website is: www.gwbrown.com.

Photo by Ellen Robson

Phantom Inmates - 1887 & 1909

Gila County Jails, Globe, AZ

by Ellen Robson

Globe, Arizona, tucked between the Apache Mountains and Pinal Mountains, was once an old mining community and now thrives as a tourist attraction. Turn of the century buildings are used for bed and breakfasts, antique stores, and small cafes. The town's first jail, as well as the one built in 1909, are still occupied—by ghosts of former inmates and employees.

The original jail was located in the courthouse that had been built in 1887. By 1909, however, a new facility had to be constructed to keep up with the growing population of criminals. The new sheriff's office and jail was built directly east of the courthouse. A catwalk was installed between the two buildings and used primarily for the transfer of prisoners from their jail cells to the courthouse. When you glance up at the catwalk, you can almost hear the distinct sound of shackles and chains of the prisoners being led across.

The ground floor of the Old Gila County Jail was used for administrative offices for the sheriff, and a steel cellblock was located in the rear. The second floor held small cells for women and juveniles while the third floor was used as an open trustee dormitory.

"Visitors who are more attuned to the various spirit activities throughout the facility, never stay long," tour guide Connie Teague explained. "And it can get pretty creepy in here when you're by yourself."

On several occasions she has felt cold spots on her left shoulder. Once, out of the corner of her eye, she caught a glimpse of what appeared to be a man peering through the glass panel that separates the offices from the jail portion of the building. Though she can't explain why, Ms. Teague feels that the ghost was of a former employee, not a prisoner. She always acknowledges the various ghosts, greeting them in the morning and saying goodnight to them when she closes up.

Some ghosts crave attention and will do anything to get it, even if it means toying with the concrete beds. The bunks were designed with a metal latch that secures the beds to the wall. To lower them, one must physically lift the latch. During a tour of the women's cell area, one visitor practically jumped out of her skin when, out of nowhere, a loud bang was heard. When she saw that one of the bunks-which she had just seen securely in place-was now in the reclining position, she decided to end her tour and made a mad dash to the nearest exit.

"We have a female ghost we call Ginney who is extremely distraught," Ms. Teague said. "Often her ghost can be heard sobbing. The legend is that she had no choice but to protect herself from her abusive husband when she killed him. Ginney shouldn't have been imprisoned in the first place."

The original jail and courthouse, which now houses the

Cobre Valley Center for the Arts, has a few ghosts of its own roaming the building. And not all of them are friendly. A medium conveyed to several staff members that the ghost on the fourth floor is a former employee who refuses to move on. This is where the judge's chambers and law library were so he was no doubt a law clerk.

Tiffany, who used to work at the Cobre Valley Center for the Arts, knows first hand how territorial this ghost is of his living quarters. The minute she stepped foot on the fourth floor early one morning, he chased her down the stairs. "He didn't chase me physically. It was his powerful, overwhelming presence that made me feel he was forcing me off of his floor," she explained. "It felt like someone very unlikable wanted me to leave, and I could feel him looking over my shoulder as I ran off."

Although the spirit doesn't welcome humans on "his" floor, he doesn't seem to mind sharing it with a fellow ghost, especially if it's an inmate who he feels is supposed to keep serving time there. The medium learned that in July of 1911, a man being held in the county jail, had been accused of raping and killing two young girls. One evening an unknown gunman hid himself in the courthouse until after closing. Aiming through a window of the courthouse and across the narrow alleyway, he shot the accused inmate as he lay in his cell, killing him instantly. The inmate conveyed to the medium that although he died in his prison cell, he feels more at home on the fourth floor of the old courthouse. He also revealed that he was sorry for committing such heinous crimes and felt he had been justly punished.

The vengeful gunman is still on the premises as well, according to the psychic. Employees say it's easy to know when he's around. He's got a cigar in his mouth at all times, and the aroma fills the room. He has been seen wearing 1920s-style clothing and a cowboy hat. On more than one occasion he has been mistaken for a visitor and asked to extinguish his cigar. When approached, he always vanishes into thin air.

The fourth floor isn't the only area that is haunted. In 1997, a visitor was browsing on the first floor when she felt someone blowing on her neck. When she turned around, however, she found herself alone. For twenty-two years, the old 16-cell jail had occupied this floor, so maybe the "someone" she felt breathing on her neck, was actually a ghostly prisoner trying to get her attention.

The third floor is now home to the Copper Cities Community Players, and the old courtroom has been converted into the troupe's theater. But the actors aren't the only ones to stage dramatic performances here. Now and then, a certain territorial ghost is known to put on quite a melodrama when someone invades his space.

The Old Gila County Jail is open for tours but it is advised that you call ahead. When you're finished with your tour, walk around the corner to the Cobre Valley Center for the Arts. Allow yourself plenty of time to explore the old courthouse. Along with the theater on the third floor, there is a very nice art gallery to visit, exhibits and a gift shop, which carries stained glass, books, hand-painted furniture, and stationery.

You can find the Old Gila County Jail at 149 E. Oak Street, Globe, Arizona 85501; Phone: (928) 425-9340. The Cobre Valley Center for the Arts is at 101 N. Broad Street, Globe, Arizona 85501; Phone: (928) 425-0884.

Ellen Robson is the author of *Haunted Highway-The Spirits of Route 66* and *Haunted Arizona-The Ghosts of the Grand Canyon State*. All sixty-six sites in Haunted Highway are open to the public. You'll read about the strange happenings occurring in Abraham Lincoln's home in Springfield, Illinois and the monkey child at the Lemp Mansion. Who would have thought a road trip down Route 66 could be so bone-chilling?

Ghostly sightings in Arizona have been around since the

1800s. *Haunted Arizona* features a collection of spirited spots from thirty-one cities, including Phoenix, Prescott, and Tucson. You'll meet Clara, a former Harvey Girl, who causes mischief at the Williams Depot and a headless man who rides the elevator at the Gadsden Hotel in Douglas.

Ellen is always chasing down ghost stories and is currently working on her third book. Every month she adds a new ghostly tale on her website at www.spirits66.com , and she invites her visitors to share their own ghostly experiences as well. You can contact her at emrobson7@aol.com.

Photo by Cindy Stavely, Old Jail Historic Tours of America

Certifiably Haunted - 1891

St. Johns County Jail, St. Augustine, FL

by Joy Nord

One rainy dreary day a young boy played upstairs near the men's cells while his father and mother followed the tour guide into a different part of the old jail. He heard someone mumbling and looked around. He was alone. The boy continued pretending to be the sheriff but heard the chatter again. This time as he walked around in wonder, he heard whistling and felt a cold breath on his neck.

He ran to his parents, able to get out only one word, "Ghosts!"

"It's possible." The tour guide nodded without excitement.

In the early 1500s, Juan Ponce de Leon had been seeking

the Fountain of Youth when he sailed northwest from Puerto Rico. He sighted land along the Atlantic Coast, somewhere between the St. Johns River and Cape Canaveral and claimed it for Spain. Because of its beautiful appearance, he named it La Florida meaning "Land of Flowers."

Almost four centuries later, railroad magnate and oil tycoon Henry Flagler began seeking new adventures and was just as impressed. As soon as he moved into the sleepy old Spanish town of St. Augustine in 1885, business started to stir. Intrigued by the climate and quaint environment, the New York native saw great potential in one of the oldest inhabited cities in the United States. He had made millions as co-founder of the Standard Oil Company with John D. Rockefeller, and he put his vast fortune to work creating a resort and playground for rich Northerners.

He embarked first upon St. Augustine and transformed it into the "American Riviera." Flagler constructed three magnificent hotels, the Ponce de Leon, the Alcazar, and the Casa Monica. He also provided money for the town's hospital, city hall, and several churches, and his funding didn't stop there. When Flagler didn't like the jail obstructing the full view of his new luxury hotels, he exchanged building lots with the city and had the jail torn down. City officials relocated the new jail farther away from town. Since Flagler financed the building, it's not hard to guess what the jail resembled – a massive Queen Anne-style stucco on brick hotel. But nothing resembled luxury on the inside, except maybe the sheriff's quarters.

Completed in 1891, the old jail housed prisoners for over 60 years. Engineered by the same company that built Alcatraz, the St. Johns County Jail was designed with cells for both males and females and could hold 72 prisoners. The men's cells consisted of two floors, with eight cells per floor, each cell having four bunks. All cells were in the center of the room with a corridor surrounding the outside.

The women's cells were on the first floor just inside the backdoor. Ironically, few women ever stayed there because, under the judge's order, female offenders were confined to house arrest. Besides the regular cells, a maximum-security area, which consisted of stockades and a torture cage, was on the backside of the building. During the prison's use, no glass was installed in the windows except in the sheriff's apartment. The solitary-confinement cell had neither windows nor bedding.

Prisoners condemned to hang were housed in a special cell from which they could watch the gallows being built beside the jail. At these gallows, many prisoners paid the ultimate price for their crimes at the end of a hangman's noose as they dangled to their death.

The sheriff's apartment, where he and his wife raised their children, was adjacent to the inmate's cells upstairs on the second floor. Victorian furnishings supplied comfort for his family, and they shared the same kitchen facilities where deputies prepared meals for the inmates. The latter consisted of strong coffee and hardtack (a mixture of flour and water, without salt, baked hard). As one prisoner stated, "It ain't so bad once you drown the weevils in the coffee."

St. Augustine's Sheriff, "Big Joe" Perry, stood six-feet-six-inches tall and weighed 320 pounds. His disposition towards his prisoners mirrored theirs regarding him. The sheriff didn't like new prisoners because, as he put it, "They have an attitude." He would tell new inmates what they should expect if they needed an attitude adjustment and describe graphically the conditions they might bring on themselves. He wouldn't tolerate any complaints from prisoners about working 16 hours a day on the new highway either.

Sheriff Perry warned prisoners that his nickname was "Always Gets His Man," and once the prisoner was behind bars, Perry had no intention of letting anyone out of jail until the new highway was completed. He would also point out to new captives that "Sure Shot Higgins," a deputy stationed up in the tower, had a reputation of not missing his target.

Such a history makes it easy to see why the old jail might harbor paranormal activity. Today management staff, tour guides, and tourists report strange occurrences within the structure such as: the sound of shuffling feet and other odd sounds, physical interaction, items being misplaced or moved, cold spots, a sensed presence when no one is around, the putrid smell of unwashed bodies and the pungent odor of "sanitary" facilities—where four prisoners per bucket had shared a cell. School children visiting the main cellblock have even seen a very large shadowy figure of a man wearing a plaid shirt.

But can these reports be authenticated?

On October 24, 2003, North Florida Paranormal Research, Inc. investigated the old St. Johns County Jail with the NBC *Today Show* crew. Matt Ferrell stated in his report, "Most of the time, when we have TV/ Radio crews at an investigation, we don't usually capture much. Having people with TV cameras running all around and people asking questions all the time usually takes away your focus on the investigation. But, in this case, even though we had media crews there, we came away with some interesting results."

Glen Baker set up a Sony Night video camera in the back on the first floor. He captured one orb outside the cellblock door from the kitchen area into the area used to house female inmates. Earlier Glen had complained to Matt of someone whistling, but inspections from the windows revealed there was no one outside or inside the vicinity other than the two men. Matt did not hear the whistling, and it wasn't recorded on the videotape at that time.

Later when the TV crew was setting up for an interview, they heard strange sounds that were not picked up by the video recorder either. But after the interview, they found that the EVP (electronic voice phenomenon) had captured what sounded like a male voice groaning as if in discomfort.

Minutes later, a man's whistling is captured on the EVP that only lasted about four seconds. All of this took place over people's conversations in the room.

With the capture of paranormal activity on still photography cameras, video cameras, EVPs, and the documentation of witnessed accounts, Jeff Reynolds certifies, "The Old Jail is authentically haunted by our standards and protocols. Our panel of field investigators, outside parties, and myself ensure credibility and have painstakingly analyzed all evidence."

Today, through guided tours, this haunted old jail exhibits strictness of incarnation during a time of heavy shackles and ball-and-chains. The old jail is listed on the Florida and National Haunted Places Register and is the site of numerous supernatural occurrences. The St. Augustine Jail is also on the National Registry of Historic Places. One of the few remaining 19th century facilities in the state, it is the oldest government building in St. Johns County Florida.

After being captivated by the jailers' stories, you can spend more time wandering through the Florida Heritage Museum at the Authentic Old Jail, which documents four-hundred years of Florida's past, focusing on the life of Henry Flagler, the Civil War era, and the Seminole Wars. The jail is located at: 167 San Marco Ave., St. Augustine, Florida, and operates daily, except on major holidays. A tour takes approximately 30 minutes. FFI: (904) 829-3800.

Ghostly evening tours are also available through Ghosts and Gravestones. This tour includes traveling the streets of St. Augustine, with "the town gravedigger" as your guide, to see other haunted sites. His stories of spirits promise to "leave you dying for more." FFI: 1-800-404-2531.

Author Joy Nord's biography can be found on page 166.

To offset the utter desolation of his cell, one prisoner hand-painted garden scenery at his window (photo by Tonya Hacker).

The Black Jail - 1892

Oklahoma Territorial Prison, Guthrie, OK

by Tonya Hacker

When we investigated the Oklahoma Territorial Prison for evidence of haunting, Tricia picked up something on her analog tape recorder; she collected an EVP (electronic voice phenomenon). This EVP is what we have labeled a responsive or reactive EVP, which indicates that one of the rumored ghosts is to be an "intelligent" haunting, not a residual.

Tricia and I were speaking about the hole in the wall that had been used for an escape attempt. The hole is now covered up with stucco. Here is what we got:

I say, "I betcha 50 bucks it was right here."

"RRRRRRIGHT!" a male voice says clearly.

The only other person around was our photographer, Todd, and it is definitely not him. The voice caught on tape is of an older male, with a deep, congested voice.

This is what we call a "Class A" EVP (highest on the scale).

Fifteen years before it earned statehood in 1907, the Oklahoma Territory was overrun with gunslingers, robbers, and notorious western outlaws. In 1892 Guthrie became home to one of the very first U.S. territorial prisons in the Midwest.

Labeled the "Black Jail" by inmates, the penitentiary with its 18-inch-thick walls of dark limestone and brick was rumored to be escape-proof back in the days of the Wild West. Intimidating to the locals, the shadowy halls of this prison detained some of America's most notorious criminals of the day. Scandalous outlaws such as the well-known Bill Doolin and his gang of murderous thieves passed through the dank cells frequently. The legendary Dalton Gang also had its last go around during the first years of the prison.

The two-story structure housed no more than ninety prisoners at a time, two levels of steel cages including the basement where the unruly convicts were held in solitary confinement. Solitary confinement was becoming a popular way "to offer treatment" to hardened criminals in hopes of curing them of their wrongful ways. At least it gave the community a sense of safety from the convicted felons being held within their township. Description of the living conditions at the prison varied. While the local newspaper reported that harsh living conditions were not the norm, other reports presented a different view. Lack of ventilation for the prisoners was the main concern to many within the community. Neither the intense Oklahoma heat nor the harsh winters played a positive role with the inmates and their well-being during their incarceration.

I visited the facility as an investigator for Ghost Haunts of

Oklahoma and Urban Legends Investigations (GHOULI). I wanted to walk through the halls and see the prison while it underwent restoration efforts, activity that tends to stir up any lingering spirits.

Employees and volunteers at the prison confirmed the rumored reports of the supernatural and paranormal activity that plagues the interiors of the prison. The sense of being followed and watched is the most common and certain feeling cited by guests. The occasional haunting murmurs that descend down the cell halls are an eerie reminder that troubled individuals resided within these walls many years ago. But when new rules for upgrading conditions for prisoners were established, the prison was found inadequate and had to close in the early 1900s.

Subsequent to that, a local chapter of the Nazarene Church adopted the building as its new home for worship, and the church occupied the building until the late 1970s. The building sat unoccupied for many more years, until a charitable foundation purchased it and opened the doors for cult members to make Guthrie their new home. Locals were always uneasy about the rituals being performed in the church. It quickly became one of the things the town mistrusted. Murder, scandal, and conspiracy were hastily attributed to the organization up until 1995.

Investigation confirmed that the foundation was not what the townspeople had first thought it to be. Its headquarters was known to harbor anti-government activists and radicals, and its motives for taking in homeless children and runaways were questionable. After the Department of Human Services declared the structure unfit for the children who lived in the compound, the doors were officially closed in the late 1990s.

The strange and unusual combination of history at this building leaves plenty of reasons why it may be inhabited by the ghostly energy and strange occurrences that people are experiencing today.

One of the most familiar spirits at the prison is assumed to be the ghost of James Phillips. In June 1907, Phillips was the first white man sentenced to be hanged at the prison for the murder of a local man. According to prison records and the State Capital Newspaper, Phillips was to die on a mid-June morning across the street of Noble Avenue. Observing diligently through his cell window he watched the local carpenters build his personal hanging gallows. Guards reported that Phillips was watching the construction with a great deal of dread and angst. Then all of a sudden, he abruptly fell backwards onto his bunk, dying instantly without a sound or even a word of warning. The coroner's report printed in the local newspapers stated nothing but, "He simply died of fright."

The ghost of James Phillips has been seen walking the corridors of the basement awaiting his demise that was to transpire the very next morning. Witnesses who pass by have reported a man peering out the lower level window. Workers and preservation volunteers have seen dark shadows on occasion, and this shadow seems to seek refuge in the cell where Phillips was rumored to have died that summer day.

Sentenced to die almost 100 years ago, is James Phillips still awaiting his death in the historical Black Jail? Is Phillips unable to realize, that in the end, he avoided the gallows of his own execution that he feared so greatly? Rumor and witness testimony holds this to be the certainty in the basement chambers of the prison.

A different ghostly tale involves a young woman. No one is certain of who she is, why she is present, and what time frame she fits in to, but a young woman's voice can be heard singing throughout the main level of the building. She wears a long printed dress and sports a large brimmed hat with gloves. The woman has only been seen by a select few townspeople. However, she has been noticed outside the prison walking the grounds and on occasion attempting to cross the street of Noble

Avenue. Drivers have been known to slow down or even stop in the middle of road as a woman makes her way across and then swiftly vanishes before stepping up to the curb.

Some locals believe the woman was nothing but a common prostitute brought in by guards to provide leisure activity for prisoners who displayed good behavior during their confinement.

Others have quite a different theory. They believe she was a prominent member of the Nazarene Church. One witness states, "She looked like a civilized woman, walking with her head high, into the church doors." The nameless woman appears on occasion, usually at dusk, and alone.

Examining the main floor of the building, I saw remnants of the old church still hanging suspended from the ceiling: rusted, pressed-tin tiles are torn and bent, a few lying on the floor of what used to be a sanctuary and worship hall. Whoever this woman is remains a mystery. Why she continues to roam the grounds, the halls, and the residually haunted path of Noble Avenue is a familiarity the locals have just accepted as part of the building's past, present, and future.

While researching the location, interviewing and spending time inside the walls of the prison, I personally witnessed a few unexplainable moments. Walking the main floor of the prison, I noticed a large hole in the floor. I stopped walking to peer into the basement and take some photos. Lightly behind me, I heard a few dragging footsteps echoing, as if they were made of sturdy leather with a distinct heel. Wearing soft sole shoes myself, I was truly startled.

Another experience caught my attention while I was in the basement photographing James Phillips' cell. I noticed what appeared to be a man walking past the window. In hopes that it was one of the volunteer workers, I rushed up the rickety stairs to interview him. Running to the front door, I stepped outside and looked up the street and all around. There was no one in sight.

Standing in the cellblock hallway of the basement, my associates, Tricia Cross, EVP specialist; Todd Hoagland, photographer; and I were startled at the clanging sound of metal hitting metal, similar to the closing of a cellblock door. Only one metal door is left in the prison, and that door was about three feet in front of us within our view. We searched for another door but were not able to locate the origin of the noise, or recreate the noise with any debris in the area. In addition to the EVP mentioned earlier, the sense of being followed and the strong sense of being watched was the most uncomfortable event we witnessed that day. There is no doubt in my mind that the Black Jail of Guthrie, Oklahoma could be one of the more haunted locations in this charmingly haunted, historical town.

As the town continues to restore historical buildings to their original splendor, the prison unfortunately is one of the last to be restored. A new roof was recently added to prevent further damage from the elements. The town of Guthrie welcomes visitors and hopes to get the Federal Prison restored to its original state so that it can become a museum and receive visitors in the near future. It has been selected for various preservation grants and federal money, but that will not be enough.

Historical researchers, history buffs, and everyone else in the town of Guthrie are anxiously awaiting the overdue renovation of the prison. For a town so full of western heritage, one can only hope that historical foundations and independent contributions continue to pour into the community. Contributions to the Federal Prison's Restoration efforts are welcome. Please contact the Guthrie Oklahoma Chamber of Commerce at (405) 282-1947.

Tonya J. Hacker, is the founder of an Oklahoma-based paranormal investigative team, www.ghouli.com (Ghosts Haunts of Oklahoma & Urban Legend Investigations). For over five years, she has researched reports of ghosts, folklore, and

urban legends in and around the area. She particularly enjoys the ghostly stories attached to haunted locations and has had considerable success in collecting EVPs, (Electronic Voice Phenomena). She has been featured on national and local television and radio. She also hosts Historically Haunting Tours in Oklahoma City along with conferences and other paranormal related events.

Being a single mother of two girls, she tries to set an example to her children to go after their passions in life no matter how obscure they may be. Ever since she was a child, her fascination with abandoned buildings, spooky tales, and the possibility of ghosts has played a major role in her life. Tonya takes pride in offering a skeptical outlook in the field while applying history and a common sense approach to paranormal research.

Outside of investigating, she enjoys spending time with her family, listening to vintage music, and making short films. As an author, she is currently writing her first book, a collection of *Oklahoma Ghost Stories*.

Photo courtesy of J.M. Cooper

Whispers Within The Walls - 1894

Montana Territorial Penitentiary, Deer Lodge, MT

by Ellen Baumler

The federal government established a territorial penitentiary at Deer Lodge, Montana in 1870. In over a century of use, the prison saw more than 27,000 men, and some women, lose their freedom and their identities. Remnants of the misguided humanity once stored inside the imposing stone walls have left an indelible impression. These traces follow the visitor's every step. Shadows loiter in the dark recesses and secret places. Visitors will tell you that there is a palpable energy thick enough to change the minds of even the most skeptical.

After prison authority passed to the state in 1889, the original federal prison buildings were gradually replaced. The present fortress-like wall, built with convict labor in 1894, is today the oldest part of the prison complex. The wall set the standard for other buildings added over time. Massive, crenellated towers chronicle a layered and violent history—witnessing more than enough bloodshed to permeate every brick and stone. One bloody incident occurred on March 8, 1908. The facility was overcrowded with 400 inmates when prisoners George Rock and W. A. Hayes attempted to escape. They fatally slit Deputy James Robinson's throat with a pocketknife and severely slashed Warden Frank Conley before officials subdued them. Both Rock and Hayes suffered gunshot wounds, but Conley carefully nursed them back to health. Then they were hanged in the prison yard as an example to the other men.

A women's prison outside the original wall and a new cellblock built inside the walls in 1912 improved conditions. Later, copper king W. A. Clark of Butte endowed a prison library and donated $10,000 for the construction of a theater. Built in 1919, it was the first theater built inside a prison in the United States. Then in 1921, Governor Joseph Dixon removed Conley as warden. While he accomplished much during his thirty-year tenure, Conley's own personal gain tainted his achievements. His once progressive institution deteriorated into a human wasteland.

In 1959, prisoners rioted. Brandishing mops soaked in flammable liquid, they took eighteen employees and five inmates hostage, killing Deputy Warden Theodore Rothe. The Deer Lodge riot made international news. The National Guard finally stormed the prison with automatic weapons, a WWII vintage bazooka, and tear gas. The two masterminds died in one of the cellblock towers, a murder-suicide; bazooka scars still mar its window.

In the 1960s, Larry Cheadle was serving a term for car

theft. He was unruly and disruptive, but the guards had special punishment for such inmates. Beneath the 1912 cellblock were six dungeon-like cells hollowed out of the bedrock known as The Hole. A mattress, a pitcher of water, a bucket for waste, and total darkness were the only amenities. On Halloween morning, 1966, guards placed Larry Cheadle below in the cell where a previous inmate had hanged himself from an overhead pipe. A guard found Cheadle dead six hours later.

The incident raised questions. Cheadle had a heart murmur, but did pipes outside the cell emit enough steam to cause overheating? The coroner found body heat present hours after death and Cheadle's internal organs were warmer than his hands. In other words, Cheadle appeared to have cooked to death. Inmates further claimed that Cheadle had been beaten and that guards removed his bloody mattress and burned it; the official report, however, included no inmate interviews.

In the prison's final decade, inmates set a fire that left the W. A. Clark Theater a burned out shell. In 1979, the state completed a modern facility west of Deer Lodge. The old prison—once home to thousands upon thousands of the state's most hardened castoffs—opened as a museum in 1980. Since then, the cells have been empty. Or so one would believe.

From 1985 to 1990, Bill Felton worked as a state corrections officer at the new Montana State Prison. One of his duties was taking trustees to their jobs in town. Some of these trustees worked doing needed maintenance on the prison museum. Many of the older inmates had done time there, and Bill had heard all their stories.

"Myth is more important than fact to the inmates," cautions Bill. "They like to gossip." But he had occasion to spend a fair amount of time with the inmates and other guards in the old facility. While he never felt threatened there, he admits that the prison has a creepy feel to it. No wonder.

Bill puts it this way, "More souls than people died in that place. Although there is plenty of death within the walls, more men came into the prison, did their time, and were released than died at Deer Lodge. While they were there, the prison took their souls. There is more despair in there than death."

For all its empty cells, Deer Lodge is reputedly an active place. Many visitors talk about hearing voices. Bill agrees. He says that in the burned out theater or in the cellblock in particular, the guards or inmates with him always seemed to talk too much and too loudly, as if they didn't want to hear what was going on in the background. But when he was in those places alone, he could hear the whispering. Bill describes the sounds as babbling. Some people can hear it, others cannot. He says you have to listen.

Museum director John O'Donnell agrees that his museum is a spiritual repository where not just the prisoners, but the guards too, have left impressions of themselves. With a background in political science and history, John has a deep sense of appreciation for the men and women whose stories are intrinsic to the prison's past—a social history ironically confined like its inmates—within the formidable stone walls. He is sensitive to places steeped in the past, and is interested in what others experience. That is why he allowed Kris Bratlien and friends, armed with some sophisticated recording equipment, to spend a night inside the walls.

What began for Kris as a high school psychology project had become an avocation; this was not his first such venture. So on this cold, dark Saturday evening in the early spring of 2005, Kris, his dad, his sister, and four friends assembled in the prison yard. Protection is essential in a place like Deer Lodge, so they said a non-denominational prayer. "We didn't want to bring anything home with us," Kris explained. John, concerned for their safety in the dark, unheated prison, gave the group a couple of two-way radios while he remained in his office with a third radio. What the group recorded proved interesting.

Kris and his friends Cody and Aaron first went to the cell at the far end of the hole beneath the 1912 cellblock. They had a night vision camera and an electronic motion detector. Kris knew that a prisoner had hanged himself in this cell, but he did not know about Larry Cheadle and the allegations of abuse. As they set up the recorder for electronic voice phenomena (EVPs), they heard footsteps out in the hallway. The moment they activated the recorder, Cody's head hit the wall. Kris and Aaron heard the sickening thud. Cody later said that he felt someone put a hand in his face and shove him. The three were shaken. John later observed that Cody seemed to have red marks on his face and neck. The bump on the back of his head brought on a migraine. Later in the evening, severe headaches plagued both Kris and Aaron as well.

The group taped in a number of places and played portions of both sound recordings and video for John. The tape made in the Maximum Security building clearly recorded women sobbing. Until John told them, Kris and the others had not known that this area was originally the 1908 women's prison. In the office where Deputy Warden Rothe died, John observed an object on the video that skittered across the floor and flew out of the camera's eye. "It was dark," said John, "and big, like a bumble bee or a butterfly. But it was 20 degrees that night in the unheated prison, and I know for a fact there were no insects in there. It was weird." The camera also recorded moving orbs, or balls of light. John observed them on the video in the Maximum Security area, around the cellblock shower, and in the hallway outside the hole. A professional videographer later confirmed that the tapes were not doctored. In the cellblock, EVPs included footsteps like those of guards in heavy boots, banging metal gates or cell doors, and the faint sounds of men whispering, or babbling. Over the course of that long night, Kris says they all observed shadows that darted out from dark places, crossing the hallways and corridors. They wondered if unexplained static on the two-way radios was someone, or something, trying to communicate with them through "white noise."

Veteran prison tour guide Marlene Olmstead is not surprised by what Kris and his friends experienced and recorded. Marlene grew up in the town of Deer Lodge and is well acquainted with the prison's tragedies. Her mother, beloved by both prisoners and personnel, worked for many years in administration inside the walls. Just before the 1959 riot, six inmates suddenly came into her office, told her to ask no questions, and escorted her out. Ten minutes later in a nearby office, the instigators murdered Ted Rothe. Rothe's daughter Phyllis and Marlene were in high school and best friends at the time.

Marlene has had her own experiences in the prison. It is comforting for her to sense that her mother—who was for so long an integral part of the facility—is still there in spirit in the office area. But other spirits are not so pleasant. One cloudy afternoon as she gave a tour for a group of thirty visitors, Marlene led them as she always did to the far north end of the 1912 cellblock. As she passed the first cell, a blast of heat hit her like a wall. No one else seemed to have this experience, but she realized that her face must have turned red; several tourists asked her what was wrong. She pretended nothing had happened, regained her composure, and proceeded past a few more cells. It happened again. A blast like a wall of heat from a fiery furnace hit her so hard that she almost fell to her knees. Then she experienced a terrible chill. She somehow managed to finish the tour. After the group had gone, Marlene went alone to retrace her steps. She walked into the north end of the cellblock, and it immediately happened again.

"The heat was so intense," says Marlene, "that it pulsated from the walls and the cells. Everything seemed to light up. I am not sure what it was, but I translated the heat as evil and rage. I knew for certain that something wanted me out of the way."

Marlene related her experience to a co-worker who only half believed her. Then about a week later, the co-worker told

Marlene that a young man had taken the tour and come into the gift shop white as a sheet. He related an identical experience. Marlene now takes her tour groups along a different route.

Marlene often opens the museum and locks it at night. Sometimes tourists have been mistakenly locked in, and so whoever is the last to leave has to make sure everyone is out of the facility. One evening as Marlene made her usual rounds, she entered the cellblock and heard men laughing and talking loudly. She yelled, "Closing in 10 minutes. I would appreciate it if everyone would please leave." There was sudden dead silence. Marlene walked all around, but there was no one in the building. She finished turning out the lights and headed to the main entrance. As she was about to walk out the door, Marlene says, "I heard someone behind me laugh. It was the most evil laugh I ever heard, but when I looked around, no one was there." She quickly stepped out and shut the door behind her, thinking, "Whoever you are, you can just stay in there."

The Old Montana Territorial Prison, used as the Montana State Prison until 1979, today is a museum where you can take either self-guided or guided tours. It is open seven days a week 8 AM to 8 PM. from May 15 to October 15 and from 10 AM to 4 PM. during the off-season. Located at 1106 Main Street in Deer Lodge, Montana 59722. FFI: 406-846-3111 or www.pcmaf.org/prison.htm.

Ellen Baumler delights in making Montana's past come alive. She has been a historian with the Montana Historical Society since 1992. Researching out-of-the-way places and their little-known stories as the State's National Register sign program coordinator led Ellen to write her best-selling first book, *Spirit Tailings: Ghost Tales of Virginia City, Butte, and Helena*(Montana Historical Society Press, 2002) and a second book of ghostly tales, *Beyond Spirit Tailings: Montana's Ghosts, Mysteries and Haunted Places*, (Montana Historical Society Press, 2005). Richly embroidered with Montana's

Photo by Katie Baumler

unique historical legacy, Ellen crafts her eerie tales around well-researched historical facts and events. But armed with a Ph.D. in English, Classics, and History from the University of Kansas, she has taught a popular college class in Montana History since 1995. Ellen's unique *History Half-Notes* airs daily on local radio stations and she has authored dozens of articles on such diverse topics as camels in Montana's mining camps, the Florence Crittenton Home in Montana, Montana's Lewis and Clark landmarks, and Butte's red light district. Ellen is also editor of *Girl from the Gulches: the Story of Mary Ronan*, honored as a Finalist Award Winner for the prestigious 2004 Willa Cather Literary Awards.

Photo courtesy of Mansfield Reformatory Preservation Society

Cathedral, Or Dracula's Castle - 1896
Ohio State Reformatory, Mansfield, OH

by Elizabeth J. Baldwin

Traveling along Route 545, looking for the Ohio State Reformatory at Mansfield, you do not expect to top a hill and see Dracula's castle, but there it stands—in all its Gothic aura. And you feel as if you have somehow warped through time and space to Transylvania.

Levi T. Scofield, the lead architect for the project, based his design on Cathedrals found in Europe, particularly those in Germany. He wanted his soaring Gothic style to encourage inmates to aspire to better things than criminal activity. Whether any did take such a lesson from the building is unknown.

Ohio State Reformatory, OSR, began as a Civil War training camp in 1861, called Camp Mordecai Bartley after a

Governor who came from Mansfield. In 1867 Mansfield was nominated as a potential site for an Intermediate Penitentiary. State officials intended it as a halfway prison for young men no longer eligible for the Boys Industrial School in Lancaster, Ohio, but not yet the hardened criminals usually sent to the State Penitentiary in Columbus.

Old Camp Mordeccei Bartley was selected as the site for the new Mansfield prison in 1885. Work on the prison was slow, but the first prisoners arrived on September 15, 1896. The 150 men were immediately put to work building the 25-foot wall surrounding the 15-acre plant. They also built the sewer system, and the facility was completed in 1910. It houses the world's largest freestanding cellblock, which is six stories high.

Some visitors claim, even before reaching the complex, to see unexplainable sights along Reformatory Road. Most of the reported apparitions, figures and objects haunt the old reformatory cemetery. However, since the cemetery is located on state owned property it can only be studied from a distance. A guard tower approximately 300 or so yards away is the best observation point.

The prison's dark, brooding presence and its history, leave little wonder why the place might be haunted. Ghost hunters consider it a favorite ground to hone their skills. Too many ghosts have been spotted to make cataloguing all of them possible. But incidents known to have happened in certain parts of the prison make them likely for serious haunting, and these are hot spots where spirits replay their troubled pasts. Participants on the tours report seeing figures and hearing voices.

Both professional and amateur paranormal researchers and ghost hunters exploring Mansfield Reformatory have obtained fascinating results. People attempting to use electronic equipment to record data and cameras to photograph events they've witnessed report an unusually high equipment failure and malfunction rate—not always because the equipment refuses to work. Perhaps more unnerving are the times when it works by itself, recording sounds and pictures the operator would not otherwise have gotten.

Visitors who take animals into certain areas have noticed strange behavior. The animals whine, cling, and act afraid or depressed. Sometimes they absolutely refuse to enter a room.

On occasion the Ohio Prison System kept death row inmates incarcerated at OSR, but while an electric chair is now on display, it is merely a replica. Not only did OSR never have such a chair, but no one was ever executed there.

Interestingly enough, it is the administrative wings that produce the most negative energies, so much so that even witnesses who profess to be unaware of presences in other areas say that here they feel as if they are being watched and even touched. They experience the strongest emotions in the warden's quarters. "The pink bathroom" has quite a disturbing atmosphere about it according to many who have been in it. Some have postulated that the wrong done in the administrative areas might have been a greater evil than what went on in the prison area proper.

At least two actual stories involved the old superintendent's quarters.

In July of 1948 two men, who had been released from OSR for "good behavior," launched into a three-day killing spree by murdering Earl Ambrose, a Columbus tavern owner. Next they stole a car and drove back to OSR where they kidnapped OSR farm superintendent John Niebel, his wife and daughter from the Superintendent's house off Route 13. These good behavior ex-cons took the family to a cornfield off Fleming Falls Road and murdered all three. After killing several more people, the "Mad Dog" killers, as the press dubbed them, were finally stopped by a roadblock. One was killed in the ensuing shootout. The other was re-arrested and eventually executed.

The other incident took place right in the superintendent's quarters on November 6, 1950. The wife of the superintendent was shot, when she dislodged a gun from an upper shelf of a closet. She died the next day in Mansfield Hospital. Nine years later, the superintendent died of a heart attack in his office. Might the ghost of his wife have visited him?

People tell about seeing two men struggling beside the pond in front of the prison. In 1926 a prison guard was shot there while attempting to stop a former inmate from trying to help a buddy escape.

The Chapel held Mass every Wednesday and showed movies at other times. Whatever ill deeds happened in these crowded situations, hunters and researchers describe the chapel as a nexus of impressions and energy.

Enormous cellblock areas manifest further sensations of otherworldly presence. Various personalities have been felt in the different cells. Since prisoners were abused and even killed by other prisoners it is not surprising that there are intense emotions left in these rooms.

Records bear out the fact that in any prison, during a period of overcrowding, several inmates are crowded into each cell. In that situation, not all the prisoners locked in at night are able to walk out in the morning.

Some prisoners died by their own hands. A few hanged themselves including one who was in the "hole" at the time. Another man stole turpentine and paint thinner from the prison furniture shop and used it to set himself on fire.

The West Wing is where "the hole," the solitary confinement cells, were located. Today, some visitors report feelings of despair and depression that almost overwhelm them. Not available to the general public today is a sub-basement, but some people passing the entrance to the area say they experience a chilling fear emanating from the opening.

In the 94 years of prison operation, 154,000 men were incarcerated there, and some never walked out. Over 200 prisoners and several corrections officers died, such as the one beaten to death with a three-foot iron bar in one of the solitary confinement cells.

In more recent times the place has served as a movie set. *Air Force One* and *The Shawshank Redemption* are but two that used the OSR for their sets. For *Shawshank Redemption*, scenes were filmed both on site and in specially constructed movie sets. For example, unlike scenes in the movie that show the cells facing each other, inmates could not look into other cells. Mansfield Reformatory's cells are back-to-back, and the cells actually face out towards narrow windows. However, another scene shows inmates in the actual Reformatory cemetery.

OSR had its share of both famous and infamous inmates. Henry Baker, a member of the Brinks Gang, served time at OSR. Gates Brown of the Detroit Tigers and Kevin Mack running back for the Cleveland Browns also did time at OSR.

Whether your purpose in visiting Old Mansfield Reformatory is to hunt ghosts, see where a favorite movie was made, or to do historical research, it is certain to provide plenty to see and do.

Mansfield Reformatory Preservation Society makes public tours available from May to October (admission) with special events in October. Ghost Hunts are $50 per person and participants must be 21 years of age or over. Ohio State Reformatory is located in Mansfield, Ohio, 66 miles northeast of Columbus. Take I-71 to Route 30 and Route 30 to Route 545. Turn left at the stop sign at the end of the ramp. The prison is just over the hill on Reformatory Road. FFI: www.mrps.org) or call: Convention and Visitor Bureau (800) 642-8282 or OSR (419) 522-2644

Author Elizabeth J. Baldwin's biography can be found on page 111.

Photo courtesy of Old Franklin County Jail and Museum

History That Never Rests - 1897

Old Franklin County Jail Museum, Winchester, TN

by Tonya Hacker

There is more to Winchester than just a diminutive, calm tourist town in the heart of Tennessee. Nestled at the foot of the Cumberland Mountains among lakes and fertile farmland, the town is no stranger to history. It is the namesake of Revolutionary War hero, General James Winchester, and has rich ties to the Civil War. It has stories to tell—many of them veiled in mystery.

Legends and secrets involving the Franklin County Jail that operated from 1897 to 1972, make facts hard to pin down, but visitors can imagine as they visit the century-old structure. Half the building was home to the sheriff and his family. The other half was the temporary home to prisoners, and lest they should be noisy, a 20-inch-thick brick wall separated the two halves.

Today the building is a museum, full of historical artifacts, collectibles, and local memorabilia. The sheriff's quarters and the jail itself are available to visitors. Seven of the original eight cells hold historical displays. The other, left as before, shows what an ordinary cell looked like.

But aside from the objects, recollections of yesteryear lurk within the halls, and the strong sensation of death and emotional torment remain forever inside the dank brick walls. Museum guides tell of strange noises that cannot be pinpointed, but they are hard to ignore, especially on a slow day when everything is quiet and still.

"When you're walking the halls of the old jail," says hostess, Ruth McNutt, "it is very common to have the feeling that someone is right behind you, and close. We always hear things that we can't explain." Familiar sounds are footsteps on the stairs and sounds of what seems like someone chipping away at the walls—reminders of men who sat within those former cellblocks. One can only imagine the anxiety they felt about their future. Would they be acquitted and set free? Or taken to the hanging tree, just yards away from the old jail?

Who are the trapped souls haunting the old Franklin County Jail? Some residents say they met their just reward for evil acts. Bits of information pull us back to the days of lawlessness, vigilante justice, moonshine, and purely irrational acts of violence and greed. Whatever happened, the Franklin County Jail, built on the rugged banks of Boiling Fork Creek, was the center of it all. Earlier jails had burned down, making it more difficult than ever to keep the peace.

In 1897, the new brick jail signaled to the people of Franklin County that law enforcement had officially arrived, and lawlessness was to be tolerated no more. Sheriff James Stewart apparently made every effort to uphold law enforcement, serving what he considered to be impartial and just treatment of inmates. Then came the now infamous triple execution that the conscientious sheriff never could forget.

Three men, hearing that money was to be found in a certain home, broke in and shot the man and his wife. The man died, but the woman lived to tell about it. The men were caught and brought to trial where they were identified and proven guilty. The judge sentenced them to death.

According to reports, Sheriff Stewart fed the convicted men their last breakfast, listened to their last wishes, and bade them farewell. He then performed the execution that sent them to a life he said was "far better off than the one we now leave."

People who knew him said the experience ruined his life, and he was never again the same. Some even suggested that any judge who issued an execution order should be the one who has to carry it out. In any case, the triple execution left four tormented souls. Could any or all of them be the ghosts that frequent the Old Franklin Jail?

Other people believe the ghosts are those of victims who were falsely charged and sentenced to death without proof of wrongdoing. People point out one case in particular, that of Henry (full name withheld out of respect for surviving family). Back in 1882, he had been accused of raping a woman. Claiming innocence, Henry asked for a fair trial and expected to get one. Oblivious to his expectations, authorities swiftly tried and sentenced him to a horrible death. He was hanged on a tree outside the jail.

Some citizens believed the unjustified hanging was based on a personal vendetta with a local townsman. To this day visitors report catching glimpses of a dark shadow that always appears to move away from them. Could this be the ghost of Henry, fearful of being taken to the hanging tree once again?

In another case a man by the name of Rolly, who murdered his wife with a shoe, was tried and convicted at the old jail. One day while he was sitting in his cell, a lynch mob broke in, dragged him out, and hanged him from a nearby tree.

Rumor has it that a playful ghost inhabits the old jail.

Objects become misplaced or moved out of order, it seems, just to annoy museum workers. They blame the playfulness on Rolly, and state that he does "nothing scary, more of a trouble than anything." It is always good to hear there are spirits with a sense of humor, even after facing unpredicted gallows.

With so many deaths and torment having taken place at the Old Franklin County Jail, no wonder there is a different kind of history to the building in addition to a showcase of inanimate historical artifacts. Bootleggers, bushwhackers, and cold-blooded killers all confined in one place and then delivered from life—whether legally or not—these are the ingredients of legend.

No doubt the unexplainable events that take place within the museum walls are those with an evocative past and a forever haunting future. Trapped in the last place where they believed they were secure could be the reasons behind those paranormal occurrences inside the dark corridors of the old jail.

Winchester is a very close-knit, religious community, where few residents believe in such things as ghosts. The next time you visit Tennessee take the short drive to Winchester outside of Nashville and don't be afraid to stop in at the Old Franklin County Jail and Museum. If you ask about the strange yet ghostly events that take place, you may not get all the details you want to hear, but you surely won't get a denial that something mysterious and sometimes sinister is going on.

The Old Franklin County Jail and Museum, listed on the National Register of Historic Places, is a popular tourist attraction. You can find it at 400 Dinah Shore Blvd. 37398, Winchester, Tennessee 37398. FFI: (931) 967-0524.

www.franklincountychamber.com

Author Tonya Hacker's biography can be found on page 189.

The Old Pen - 1901-1981

Wyoming Frontier Prison Museum, Rawlins, Wyoming

by Joan Upton Hall

By 1900 when Wyoming achieved statehood, residents were determined to send a clear message to all outlaws that crime would no longer be tolerated. What's more the citizens would take extreme pleasure in punishing anyone who didn't heed the message. The "Gray Bar Hotel," otherwise known as Wyoming State Penitentiary, opened its cells for business in 1901, immediately setting up the climate for violence. No wonder the Old Pen eventually became a haunting ground.

You might say this was one of the first equal-rights locations for women. While most hoosegows separated women's cells from men's, this one provided no such privacy. Woven strap-iron was the best curtain they had. The crimes of these twenty-three women ranged widely. Annie Groves, for instance, had merely tried unsuccessfully to shoot the man who had knowingly infected her with an incurable disease. On the other hand, seventeen-year-old Anna Bruce, had methodically baked poison into her daddy's plum pie.

When you visit the museum gift shop, be sure to pick up these books: *Petticoat Prisoners of Old Wyoming,* by Larry Brown, which chronicles each woman's story, and *Savory Recipes by Unsavory Characters*. Plum pie, anyone?

I leave it to you to decide which of the next two topics is most horrendous: the do-it-yourself hanging contraption or Governor Osborne's fashion statement.

In 1892 a carpenter from Cheyenne named J.P Julien invented a hanging device that forced the hanging victim to initiate the job himself rather than troubling a law enforcer to do it. The moment the prisoner stepped on the trapdoor, a water valve opened, causing a system of pullies to open the trap. The prisoner would then drop, but not far or fast enough to break his neck. Nine prisoners "committed suicide" on the Julien gallows, all by suffocation, before the gas chamber replaced it as the approved execution method.

One man sentenced to hang earned himself a different method. This cattle-rustling, train-robbing murderer named Big Nose Parrot beat up a guard and tried to escape. Infuriated, a mob broke him out of his cell and lynched him to a telegraph pole. Dr. J.E. Osborne, M.D., took possession of Parrot's body, sawed off the top of his skull, and examined the brain for abnormalities. After none was found, things went from weird to macabre. The skull became a gift to another doctor to use for a doorstop. Then the "good doctor" had Parrot's skin peeled off, tanned into leather, and made into a pair of shoes and a medicine satchel.

Apparently, this all met with voter approval since Osborne was elected governor and wore his human-skin shoes for special occasions. It will not surprise you to learn, therefore, that earlier he had been elected as Mayor of Rawlins and went on later to become a U.S. Congressman. You have to wonder if he took that doorstop to Washington with him.

If you're up to it, you can see the shoes and skull on display at the museum. Besides the very reasonably priced prison tours, the museum staff offers special events throughout the year such as "The Big House Craft Bazaar" in December, and once a year a chance for a few lucky folks to spend a night "Locked Down" in a cell. You even get a cell to yourself. Unless some restless spirit has other ideas.

Museum director Tina Hill doesn't hesitate to say, "We've officially been declared haunted." Various paranormal investigating teams have reports on their websites replete with photos of orbs. At least one site provides audios of sounds and EVPs and describes other paranormal phenomena. These days, the Old Pen serves as Wyoming Frontier Prison Museum. It is located at 500 W. Walnut ST., Rawlins, Wyoming 82301. You may contact the staff at: (307) 324-4422. www.rawlins-wyoming.com/old_pen.htm for seasonal hours.

Author Joan Upton Hall's biography can be found on page 146.

photo by Shelley Andrews

Misery Seeks Company - 1909
Caldwell County Jail, Lockhart, TX

by Shelley Andrews

It's been said that spirits appear in places where there has been great happiness or great misery. The jail in Lockhart, Texas falls squarely in the latter category. Folks in the town know that for the last 125 years they've had more to worry about than mere criminals escaping their local calaboose. And those same lawbreakers incarcerated within the red brick structure have had more to keep them awake than mere locked cells—in the form of menacing specters.

If looks can conjure ghosts, the jail in Lockhart deserves each and every persistent tale told about it. Set behind an aging iron fence of peeling paint and gothic spires, the place whispers malevolence. The castle-like building's serrated roof line looks like a battlement, complete with a small center tower—but more about the tower later.

The building, built in 1908-09 as the fourth jail for Caldwell County, possesses one saving grace. As a rare surviving example of Norman castellated jail architecture, it has been declared a Texas Historical Landmark. The first, an unassuming log building built on the same site in 1855, had burned to the ground in 1858. The basement of the courthouse served as the jail until a third was begun in 1873. This downtown building of limestone was in use until the citizens voted on the issuance of bonds designated for building a new jail for reasons that will follow.

This fourth jail, on the corner of South Brazos and East Market Street, makes a perfect setting for a good ghost story, the unseen and equally, the unbelievable. Stories virtually hover and flit about the tall structure that, until 1982, was a working jail, housing prisoners. And once inside, your unsettled feeling only grows. Wooden floorboards creak and echo as you step into the first floor rooms where the sheriff made his home. Up a flight of steep narrow stairs, you come to a heavy metal door with flaking paint vying for space amidst the rust. Inside the cellblock the ceiling seems strangely low, or quite possibly it's the feeling of oppression bearing down. Perhaps it's due to the cells themselves, which are so small a man could go crazy locked up for very long.

In the narrow hall, another flight of stairs leads to the third floor where there are more cells and a large room for showers. On this floor, in the hallway, the ceiling rises up to the height of the tower room—the place where vicious or troublesome prisoners spent time in solitary confinement. It is in this open area on the third floor that a gibbet once hung. Maybe it was there to remind prisoners of the possibility of death and so to act as a deterrent. Or, perhaps it quietly and effectively served its designated purpose. It remains a mystery and whether or not the gallows was ever used. It was removed in the 1930s when electrocution became the favored form of putting criminals to death.

The third jail had possessed no gallows, but during the time it was in use, if you were caught and convicted of murder in Caldwell County, you swung for it. One such man was Bill Davis who was scheduled to meet his death by "lack of breath." Davis, a black man, had been found guilty of murdering another black man, Dolly Hudspeth. He appealed, but the verdict was upheld. Meanwhile, he spent his time giving interviews to newspapermen detailing how he shot Hudspeth and writing letters to his wife confessing to the crime. While in jail he could hear the hammer of wood as a gallows went up on an empty plot of land at the corner of South Brazos and East Market Street.

On the 13th of November, Lockhart began filling with people. It was a crowd-drawing spectacle, the first legal hanging in the county. Reports state that up to five thousand people came to see the brutal killer meet the rope of justice. They pressed against the barrier that surrounded the scaffold and waited until he was brought from the jail in a wagon surrounded by one hundred guards.

Davis did not disappoint. He mounted the platform and had a last confession read. In it, he exonerates all those he'd formerly named as fellow conspirators in his jailhouse interviews. It's clear by his words that he feared retribution by his former cohorts, and though he would soon be out of their reach, his wife, children, and extended family would not be.

He then had his arms pinioned to his sides as he began a hymn. The African-American people within the crowd joined in. Reports say their wild voices rose upward and had many in the crowd shaking their heads nervously. Davis then said goodbye accompanied by the eerie howling of the women and the screaming of the men. He stepped on the trap, the black cap was put up, the noose adjusted, and the drop fell. Fourteen minutes later, his body was cut down and put in a coffin for burial.

But had they really seen the last of him?

The third jail certainly hadn't seen its last prisoner and soon became the talk of the town. After the hanging of Davis, another man was hanged behind the jail according to "justice meted out illegally by Judge Lynch." In 1886 Porter Sorrelle was murdered while in the jail. The place was emptied and rumors swirled up and down the streets like a March wind. People said they heard things when going past. A few brave souls ventured closer one Saturday night and heard the clanking of chains and a voice groaning in agony. A pistol shot rang out and the group ran. The Marshal was located and went with a group of men to investigate. He found the place locked and empty, just as he'd left it.

A gathering crowd went back to the jail in the safety of numbers. As they drew near, shackles clanked from within the darkness. Another pistol shot exploded. One man could take no more and ran but the rest held their ground. As midnight drew near, a glowing man and woman walked from the building. Their feet did not touch the ground. Blood chilled to the bone, the crowd broke ranks and scattered into the night. Word spread and townsfolk shunned the place. It remained empty for a time. No one wanted anything to do with the place where spirits stalked the halls at the witching hour.

After residents voted in a new jail, the old one was taken apart stone by stone and sold. But they didn't rid themselves of the veritable ghostly inhabitants. The nearby new structure was tenanted before a single prisoner set foot in it. The clanking of leg irons dragging with each step sounded with awful regularity. The groaning of someone in the deepest despair echoed sadly through the building and pistol shots shook the quiet, dropping anyone within hearing distance.

Having gone to great expense, the townspeople refused to abandon this fourth jail, the one still standing today, despite voices speaking when no one was there, and a woman's laugh rising from the living quarters on the first floor even though no women were present. Other times, while going about his duties, the Sheriff would hear footsteps and look around the corner or into the front hall—only to find it empty. Bumps and knocks echoed throughout. Cold and hot spots baffled prisoners, workers, and visitors, and occurred anywhere and everywhere within the afflicted walls. Some reported feeling the touch of an invisible hand.

At present, the building's spooky ambiance and stories have drawn ghost hunters like a magnet to steel. In the effort to document the strange happenings, they toured the now mostly empty building using day and night vision cameras and recording devices. They found strange smells: floral perfume, urine, and feces. Sounds came from the cells: bumps, bangs and the report of a gunshot. Pictures taken appear to contain evidence of something. A vortex and one orb are present on still shots. Several moving orbs were found in the cell sealed for the investigation. These objects were not visible to the naked eye.

Though freed long ago, by one method or another, the insistent inmates refuse to go. Is Bill Davis' spirit firing a six-shooter into a chink in the wall as he spies his prey, replaying again and again his awful crime? Did the other men, murdered by mob or man, leave something behind after deaths of horrible violence? Or could some of the spirits be left over from that first log jail that burned down? One fact remains. The permanent prisoners are not going anywhere. In a place now filled with shadows and remnants of the past, they have yet to "give up the ghost."

The structure, at 315 East Market Street, now houses Caldwell County's Historical Museum and is open to the intrepid public on Saturdays and Sundays, 1-5 PM.

Shelley Andrews is a freelance writer and devoted student of history. She has membership in and serves several organizations dedicated to the preservation of Texas history,

including the Daughters of the Republic of Texas, Alamo Defenders Descendants, and the Children of the Republic of Texas. She enthusiastically tramps through spooky graveyards, intriguing ruins, dusty attics and courthouse basements in an effort to bring the past to life. She lives in Texas and can be visited online at shelleyandrews.com.

Special appreciation goes to Alamo City Paranormal investigators from San Antonio. Visit: www.lonestarspirits.org

The author took this photo before his encounter.

A Personal Encounter - 1909 (est.)

Courtland Jailhouse, Ghost Town In AZ

by Billie L. Stephens

Dust swirled around the rental car as my wife and I drove down the dirt road from Gleeson, Arizona over to the ghost town of Courtland. The noonday sun beat down on the metal roof with unrelenting heat. I swerved suddenly to miss a snake lying in the middle of the road.

"Was that a rattlesnake?" my wife, Stacy, asked as she looked up from the road map. She had grown up in Midland, Texas and knew plenty about desert snakes.

"I think it was. I didn't get a good look at it." I didn't commit myself one way of the other about the snake. "How much farther do we have to go?"

"Uh-oh, you've got to turn around. That was the wrong turn back there about a mile."

Only two ways to turn at the intersection where the main road had come to a dead end, and I had made the wrong choice. I picked a wide space in the road and turned the rental around, flipping the air conditioner up a notch.

"Tell me again. Why are we going off into no-man's land?" my wife asked.

"Research. Courtland was a mining boom town back in the early 1900s. It had four major mines there with the main ones being the Copper Queen and the Great Western. If I'm going to write about it, I need to get a feel for the area."

"What do you expect to find?"

"Don't know, but there was a General Store, Crescent Cafe, post office, newspaper office, theater, butcher shop, ice cream parlor, pool hall, and a Wells Fargo office there at one time. Oh, yeah, and a concrete jailhouse. Read that most of the buildings were razed or pushed down, but there should be some foundations and stone walls left standing." I hoped this wouldn't be a snipe hunt.

"Funny, you didn't say anything about a saloon. Didn't most of these towns have bunches of saloons and bawdy houses?" Stacy asked.

"Hum, now that you mention it..." I chuckled. "But, no, I haven't read anything about it."

"Looks like something up on the right just ahead of us." Stacy pointed.

I slowed down as we approached some old remains of a stone building. We hadn't seen a car for the last half hour, but I put on my blinker, pulled over to the right shoulder, and stopped.

We got out of the car and wandered in and around the crumbled structures. You couldn't really tell what type of building each had been the way the stone from the walls had been strewn around. Only the corners that were stuck together with concrete still stood. After a while Stacy wandered off toward another structure and I followed. Lead bullets from a present day pistol littered the ground, and I didn't want her meeting up with the shooter. But we were soon to forget human threats.

The demolished buildings were quite a distance apart, and you couldn't visualize what the town had actually looked like back in its hey-day. Pieces of rusty pipe stuck out of the ground here and there, and I remembered reading that they had piped water into the town. I also found several wide shafts that must have been mine openings at one time.

"Look over there," Stacy called and craned her neck to see a building that was almost intact.

I followed her gaze and saw a small concrete building with just minor damage. The front door frame was broken, and there weren't any windows down low, only barred openings close to the top. It was dilapidated, but what would you expect from a building almost a hundred years old? I worked my way over toward it, taking a few pictures as I went. Stacy dropped back behind me, growing strangely quiet.

"See those bars in the windows. I bet this was the town jail house," I said as we neared it from the side.

I strode on around to the front and entered it with Stacy practically on my heels.

"What was that?" Stacy grabbed my arm.

"What?" I had been looking at the walls and ceiling of the old jailhouse.

"That sudden draft. Didn't you feel that cold breeze when we came in?"

"Not really." I had no sooner answered, than the hair on my neck suddenly stood up, and a prickle ran down my spine. I glanced around the room, but there wasn't anything in the small building but Stacy and me.

"I don't like it in here. It's spooky." Stacy hugged her arms.

I whirled around. "Yeah, I just felt like something walked up behind me."

"Like someone ran his fingers lightly up my back." Stacy shivered.

"No. More like somebody you don't like suddenly walks up behind you."

"Let's get out of here. I don't like it." Stacy turned to walk out, but she halted in the doorway. "Bill, look!"

I peered in the direction Stacy was staring. Bees swarmed around a limb of a scrubby tree in front of the jailhouse. They were flying between us and the open field.

"That wasn't there when we came in here was it?" I asked.

"I don't remember seeing it, but I was looking in here to be sure there weren't any snakes or anything,"

Surely one of us would have noticed. They didn't just materialize out of thin air.

"How are we going to get out of here?" Stacy asked. "It looks like there are more now. Could they be killer bees?"

"I don't know. Killer bees are all over the southwest." My skin crawled at the thought. With my allergy to bee venom, would I be able to get to my first aid kit soon enough? The air was growing dark with bees. The swarm on the tree had grown in size, and a few were beginning to fly in and out of the jailhouse.

"We'd better figure something quick or they'll be in here with us."

I looked around the room to see if there was an opening that I had missed, but it only had the one access point. "Okay, here's what we do. Roll your sleeves down, button your top button on your blouse, put on your sunshades, and pull your cap down as far as you can. We'll run out and to the left to miss the main swarm. As soon as you get to the car, get inside, slam the door, and start swatting any bees that are on you."

"Is it unlocked?"

"No, but I'll hit the button as soon as we get close."

"This doesn't look good," Stacy said as she buttoned up. "You get in the back seat in case you get stung. I'd hate for you to start driving and have a reaction. You could have a major reaction if you're stung very many times."

"I hope I don't get stung at all. Watch it, there's more in the room now," I said.

Then I felt a coldness pass over me and I suddenly shuddered. The room shadowed a little like someone was standing in the doorway.

"Look Bill, the bees have flown outside."

Stacy was right. We had the room to ourselves now—or did we? The silhouette of a man stood in the doorway. It looked like an old man, bearded and with a slouch hat on. He seemed to be gesturing for us to follow him. I squinted at him, not sure I wasn't imagining it.

But Stacy was staring in that direction too. Her face was white and her mouth was agape.

"Do you see that?" Stacy stammered.

"Yes, and I think he wants us to follow him."

"Well, the bees are avoiding him. Let's follow and see if they stay away."

"I guess we don't have much choice."

I stepped forward and pulled Stacy behind me, and as we came forward, the man moved out of the jailhouse. The bees moved back out of the path of this apparition. He walked out in front of the jail and back down the path towards the bee swarm. I followed him with Stacy right behind me.

"Get closer." Stacy pushed me forward a little. "The bees are beginning to fill back into the space. Stay closer to him."

I moved closer to the man, and Stacy was right up against my back. The ghost kept walking and the bees continued to part from his path. As we approached the main swarm I began to get nervous, but the old man walked right on down the path.

The bees seemed to quiet down, and the hum of the mass lowered. I watched the swarm closely but they didn't pay any attention to Stacy or me as we crept past them. They were still quiet and they seemed to be dispersing.

After we got about 30 feet past the swarm, the ghost stopped and turned to us. He swept his arms as if gesturing us to proceed on past him. We stepped up and around him and hurried about 10 feet farther before I stopped and looked around. He was watching us and then waved, turned, and walked back towards the jail house, fading as he went. He had totally disappeared before he reached the bee swarm.

I looked over at Stacy and she was still watching the path towards the old jail.

"Do you believe that?" she asked. "I've never seen anything like it before, and I certainly don't believe in ghosts. But I can't explain that."

"Well, I don't care what it was. We are now safely out and past that swarm. Let's get out of here before they start flying again." I took Stacy's hand and led her to the car. We lost no time leaving the old Courtland Jailhouse. I still don't know what we actually saw, but whatever it was knew we were in danger and needed help.

When I got home to Lampasas, Texas, I started researching to see if there was anyone murdered and/or who had died in the old Courtland Jail. I have yet to find any documented deaths that could explain the presence of a ghost still taking care of the jailhouse. Whoever he was, he probably saved my life.

Courtland was a mining town with more saloons than churches in early 1909 until about 1920. The abandoned jailhouse, extensively used in the town's hey day, was still standing in the ghost town when we were there. It can be found by turning north on Ghost Town Trail, one mile east of Gleeson, Arizona, which is 15 miles east of Tombstone. It is located in the foothills of the Dragoon Mountains.

Billie L. Stephens, Ph.D. is an author living in Copperas Cove, Texas and travels across the southwest extensively doing research for the Western stories that he writes. Billie is a retired Army officer and earned a Bronze Star during Desert Storm/Shield. He now works for the US Government fielding new technology for the US Army. He has three books published, two westerns and a supernatural. *Coastal Del Rey*, and *Mesa De Lagrimas* are tales of the old west during the 1870s. The first is the story of a man after the Civil War as he drifted across the West to the Coastal Del Rey Mountains. *Mesa De Lagrimas* is the sequel and takes the hero down to Texas as he works for a railroad survey team and ends up as a Texas Ranger. *The Dome of Evil* is a current day supernatural mystery. You can preview the books and the life of this author at: http://Stephensbooks.bizland.com .

Eternally Looking Out To Sea - 1936

Old Port Orford Jail, Port Orford, OR

by Herb Holeman

Port Orford is a quaint fishing village on the rugged Oregon coast where one of the most popular tourist landmarks is a little abandoned jail. Peering into its dank interior, one senses a lingering presence. And, from time to time, visitors report eerie sounds, flickering lights and shadows emanating at night from the dilapidated building. Locals shrug away such claims as easily explainable. The little jail faces west, with an open view of the Pacific Ocean a few hundred yards away. A setting sun on the ocean's horizon could account for a glint of light within the cells, couldn't it? And at night, a reflection from the headlights of a passing car on Highway 101, which passes through the village, could account for the phenomenon, couldn't it?

As for sounds, skeptics point out that the cave-like interior of the little jail is open to nature's elements that pass through its rusted window bars. Gale force winds and heavy rains often lash the village. In fact, road signs warn the inhabitants and visitors alike that the port is located in a Tsunami area.

In any case, there is little in the jail's history to suggest ghostly phenomenon. Yet one has to wonder why the reports are simply dismissed. Village records reveal the little jail was built in 1936 in the civic center during the boom days of Port Orford—busy times for the local timber and commercial fishing industries. Local fishermen worked out of the port's pocket size harbor and brought in crab, salmon, shrimp, and bottom fish to busy dock-based canneries. The large scale logging industry produced massive quantities of locally milled wood and shipped out millions of board feet of lumber a year.

By the late 1950s activity reached its peak, and in the words of old timers, Port Orford was a "wild town." The only stories passed down by the townspeople about the little jail are more humorous than ominous. When boisterous loggers and fishermen gathered in the local bars after a day of arduous work, heavy drinking was the outcome. A steady number of patrons spent the night in the city jail as the result of the charge, "drunk and disorderly."

Such was once the predicament of a sole prisoner in the little jail, so his cohorts conjured up a plan to break him out. That night, a giant logging truck pulled up in front of the jail. The lumberjacks spilled out of the cab and wrapped heavy chains around the window bars of the prisoner's cell. The bars ripped away with little effort.

Interestingly, a court later found the jail breaker not guilty of escape since, at the time of his trial, Port Orford had no statute forbidding jailbreaks. As it happened, such a law would soon become unnecessary. The boat dock collapsed in 1961, sending millions of board feet of local lumber into the water, and although it was replaced, it was the beginning of the end of

Port Orford's heyday.

Depletion of forest timber forced local mills to shut down. Fishermen found the local waters fished out. With the local economy declining, the city fell on hard times, and the little jail was condemned in 1965.

The once civic center, just an open field, the little jail has been abandoned since then. With its rusty steel door securely padlocked and the cell bars held fast, it was not possible for anyone to gain entrance.

Over the years, discussions ranged from tearing the jail down to moving it. Then, in May 2005, the community decided to restore the little jail and preserve it as an historical landmark. City officials used bolt cutters to remove the old padlock from the door. The soil and grass blocking the doorway was removed and the steel door, coated with rust, creaked open. Inside its darkened interior, a ghostly presence, if any, went unnoticed.

Still, future visitors will be able to view the little jail. A restoration fund has been established to return the jail as it appeared in the prime of old Port Orford. Still, those eerie sounds and lights will no doubt continue, whatever the cause.

The little jail is located on Jefferson St. just as you enter the village from the south and can be seen from the highway as it is on open land a block away. FFI: Port Orford & North Curry Chamber of Commerce, P.O. Box 637, Port Orford, OR 97465, or any of these websites: portorfordchamber.com, www.protorfordnews.com, or the site dedicated to restoration of the little jail: http://oldcityjail.com.

Herbert Holeman, Ph.D. is a criminologist, and by avocation, is both a mystery writer and avid mystery reader. He is an active member of the Mystery Writers of America. His criminal justice pursuits include attending the School of Criminology at the University of California, Berkeley, and law enforcement service in beat policing, criminal investigation,

crimes studies, and criminal behavioral research. He has served as a bureau chief in the California Department of Justice.

Photo courtesy Southwest Ghost Hunters Association

Residue From A Riot - 1956

New Mexico State Penitentiary, Santa Fe, NM

by Joy Nord

No place played a bigger part in the Wild West mystique than Santa Fe, New Mexico, and like other frontier territories, it opened a federal prison before it ever became a state. But events there paled in comparison to those that followed in the 1956 "Old Main."

In 1884 the pioneer law enforcers: U.S. Marshals, county sheriffs, attorneys, and judges banded together to establish the New Mexico Territorial Penitentiary located on Cordova Road in Santa Fe. The original buildings consisted of a solid limestone structure measuring 77 x 55 feet wide, with a two-story cell house on the north side that measured 104 x 45 feet and contained 104 ventilated cells.

To celebrate the completion of New Mexico's first public building large enough to house social events, over 400 of Santa Fe's most illustrious citizens gathered to eat, drink, and dance the night away. Socializing at the prison did not stop with the magnificent housewarming. For more than 66 years the facility accommodated such galas as parties and weddings.

A wooden stockade surrounded the six-acre institution until 1899. When H.O. Bursum, a former sheriff of Socorro County, assumed the responsibilities as superintendent of the penitentiary, he replaced the walls with solid brick and constructed seven guard towers. New cell houses and other extensive improvements doubled the capacity. Before Superintendent Bursum's arrival the inmates used a wooden, horse-powered machine to manufacture brick. However, through Bursum's business dealings and influence, a modern steam plant replaced it, which could produce 30,000 bricks a day. One could say the prisoners inadvertently built a wall around themselves.

The historic prison remained in use until 1956, and in its last years, the buildings deteriorated beyond repair. Therefore, the historic 72-year-old structure, whose underground isolation cells had proved cruel and inhumane, closed down, and the facility was demolished a few years later.

Today St. Francis Drive divides the former prison grounds and two gleaming three-story office buildings that stand on the site where proud citizens once celebrated—and prisoners suffered. In two nearby cemeteries, prairie dogs dig up the bones from buried inmates and pioneers who weren't given the luxury of a coffin. Are these the spirits that roam St. Frances Drive in the darkness of night? Or the spirits that dwell in the shiny office building, producing cold spots throughout its interior, and causing elevators to malfunction, and items to disappear? When you stop dead-in-your-tracks from a rattling noise, as you walk through the graveyard, is it the ghostly sound of prisoners in chains, or rattlesnakes that live amongst the dead?

In 1956 the New Mexico Corrections Department built the New Mexico State Penitentiary out of town. But by 1980, the early days of outlawry had escalated to drug wars within the prison walls. On February 2, a prison riot started. It ended as the second worst prison riot in our nation next to that at Attica. The rebellious inmates had no plan, nor leadership, nor goals.

The riot began shortly before 2 AM Saturday morning when four guards entered dormitory E-2 on the south side of the prison. The dormitory doors and halfway gate that led into the prison control room were unlocked, a violation of prison security procedures, thus allowing inmates to overpower the arriving guards. Inmates rushed through the open doors of their medium security dormitory and within moments captured four more guards. After confiscating keys, inmates freed fellow prisoners and then stormed through an open grill gate into the administration area. As they rushed down the main corridor, they broke the shatterproof glass at the control center. The guard on duty fled, leaving behind the keys that opened most of the prison gates and doors. Enraged convicts had gained access to "The Main," a penitentiary building where 25 correctional employees supervised and cared for 1,157 male inmates.

A nightmare of violence broke out within the prison walls. First inmates senselessly set fires and ripped out plumbing fixtures. Other prisoners raided the infirmary to recommence their drug habit.

But when prisoners started to seek out their enemies, and found them, the demons of hell broke loose. Around 8 AM, inmates gained access to tools and headed for cellblock four, which had isolated the "snitches" and other inmates in the protective segregation unit. The fates of the pursued came to a horrendous end as the rioters used power tools to decapitate the snitches and several other inmates. Raging inmates tied sheets together and hanged another fellow inmate. Others used propane torches to burn their victims to death on that cold February day.

Both the State Police and National Guard were dispatched to the penitentiary. However, restoring order fell primarily upon the police. With the perimeter secure, prison officials negotiated with inmates throughout the weekend for the release of hostages and the surrender of inmates. Eventually inmates made eleven demands, mostly regarding prison conditions like overcrowding, educational services, inmate discipline, and improvement of the food.

By Sunday, February 3, at 1:30 PM, 36 horrendous hours

after the prisoners began the siege, the violence subsided, and the State Police and National Guard reclaimed the penitentiary without resistance. Inside the charred-shell-walls, the police found 33 mutilated and slaughtered inmates, most of them from the segregation unit. Medical personal treated over 100 inmates and eight guards, suffering from stab wounds, beatings, and anal rapes. The penitentiary's property damage totaled over $25 million.

After the riot one inmate wrote a letter to his attorney saying, "Everyone seems to dread the event and disappearance of the National Guard and State Police. We all seem to have the feeling that mass punishment is coming sooner or later."

He was right. But, the punishment didn't happen through the living. It emerged from the bedeviled spirits of the dead. Throughout the years, psychic vibrations resonate from the Main unit of New Mexico's State Penitentiary, a constant reminder of great pain and suffering that once took place on the premises.

On October 27, 2002, a team from SGHA (Southwest Ghost Hunters Association) and KZZR 94 Rock radio station arrived to investigate the paranormal claims. They recorded activity throughout the prison, but the most active sections consisted of cellblocks 3 and 4, the tool room, and the laundry room.

In cellblock 3, the maximum-security ward, which also included the solitary confinement cell, the team set up a video camera. They reported activity such as doors opening and closing by themselves, unexplainable noises, and lights turning off and on without any assistance.

Upon entering cellblock 4, the area that housed the "snitches," a person can see scorch marks engraved on the floor where rioters used power tools to butcher and torch their enemies. Similar activity occurred in this cell as in cellblock 3. Throughout the years, several murders had taken place in the laundry room prior to the riot of 1980. Located in a maze of corridors that lie beneath the prison cells, these corridors linked to the gas chamber, mechanical rooms, and the tool room where the inmates stole propane torches and other tools. Members of the ghost hunting team experienced discomfort in this area. Whispers were heard and unusual human-shaped shadows seen. The investigation team took over 800 photographs throughout the main unit. EVPs (Electronic Voice Phenomena) reveal sounds lurking within the prison walls. The team asked a number of questions, which received no response. Others did:

Q.: "Would you like to be somewhere else?" A.: "Playing golf."

Q.: "Are you alone?" A.: "Twenty."

In July 1998, with the opening of the third facility across the street from the riot site, Governor Gary Johnson slammed the doors shut to the Main Unit. Now, three separate facilities form the complex, Level V, Level VI, and Level II.

On my visit to the penitentiary in February, 2005, I wasn't allowed through the prison gates for security purposes. But, I did interview the guard at the main gate. When I asked him if he had ever been in the main unit, he replied, "Yes, I got the creeps. As soon as I walked through the doors, I could smell the death. I won't ever want to go into that place again, especially alone."

Within months after the closing of the Old Main, the film industry transformed the riot site into a "film village" offering low cost rentals and facilities for production companies. Among other movies made on location, have been *All the Pretty Horses* and *The Longest Yard*. The facility is fifteen miles south of Santa Fe on Highway 14.

Whether reality or fantasy, when it comes to prison violence, villains and victims are plentiful, but heroes are few.

Old Main is not open to tours, but those interested in filming on site may contact the New Mexico Film Office at: 800-545-9871 or www.nmfilm.com. FFI: Southwest Ghost

Hunters Association website: www.sgha.net/nmsp.html.

Author Joy Nord's biography can be found on page 166.

Last Words From The Editor

Well, are you ready to go to jail yet? If you've enjoyed reading these stories as much as I did collecting them, you might even find other jails to visit that we missed. The U.S. is a big country, and a book can have just so many pages.

Sad though, isn't it, that all these ghosts can never earn a pardon. Few of even the worst criminals deserve eternity. And what about the ghosts who committed no crime at all. Law enforcers. Various patriots as in the Palace of Governors in Santa Fe, Charleston, and Fort Delaware. The children incarcerated with their mothers for aiding and abetting family members as in Independence, Missouri and Gonzales, Texas. The slaves as in Equality, Illinois. And the falsely accused anywhere.

We can only hope these hauntings are "residual" instead of "intelligent," which must be sad for them. Different ghost experts have different theories about how this works, but here's the general scoop. Residual spirits keep repeating the same actions and sounds, unaware of living people. They do not endanger or try to interact with you, and you can take comfort in understanding that the spirit isn't present to suffer the emotion.

Intelligent spirits interact with the living, manifesting their presence by way of scent (such as perfume or smoke), answering you (either audibly or, more often, on tape), touching you, blowing on your skin, using force on you, or even playing tricks on you. Occasionally they may become visible. Reasons they remain "on this side" or fail to go on to another plane of existence might be: unfinished business (making peace with someone? getting revenge? protecting someone or something? bidding a farewell?). Or perhaps they don't realize they're dead.

Photographs pick up orbs, streaks of light, and other things that can't be explained. Since a picture is reputed to be worth a thousand words, take a look at these two.

The above photo by Trevor Knutson, who captured this image of an orb while taking a tour of the Old City Jail at Charleston, South Carolina (Courtesy of Bull Dog Tours).

In Buffalo Gap, Texas, Paulina Murnahan (of Central Texas Ghost Search), captured this face coming out of a wall while she was simply snapping shots of an area indicating "activity" by the instruments. I can attest to the wall panel looking quite ordinary to the eye.

For the prisons and jails you read about that have been movie sets, renting the movie to see them is fun. But when you go to the real locations, don't be surprised if you encounter images that aren't reeling off movie film.

In the Introduction, I called myself a casual observer regarding ghosts, but of course nobody is. The very mention of the word prompts people to do one of three things: (A) laugh derisively (not open to any evidence that questions what they "know"); (B) perk up with interest (eager to hear alternative "factual" evidence and often ready to share an unexplainable experience of their own); or (C) squirm in discomfort (ready to go either way but hoping against hope there's no such thing). The fact that you picked up this book very likely puts you in category "B."

For that, if we should ever meet, let's hope I'm either still among the living or an "intelligent" spirit. In either case, maybe we can swap a tale or two.

Look for these titles in the *Haunted Encounters* series:

Haunted Encounters:
Real-Life Stories of Supernatural Experiences

ISBN 0-9740394-0-3

Haunted Encounters:
Ghost Stories From Around the World

ISBN 0-9740394-1-1

Haunted Encounters:
Personal Stories of Departed Pets

ISBN 0-9740394-2-X

Haunted Encounters:
Departed Family and Friends

ISBN 0-9740394-3-8

Other Books by Atriad Press:

A Ghost in My Suitcase
A Guide to Haunted Travel in America
by Mitchel Whitington

ISBN 0-9740394-5-4

Fear
A Ghost Hunter's Story
by Kriss Stephens

ISBN 0-9740394-4-6

A Paranormal Casebook
Ghost Hunting in the New Millennium
by Loyd Auerbach

ISBN 1-9331770-4-7

Spadefish: On Patrol With A
Top-Scoring World War II Submarine
by Stephen L. Moore

ISBN 1-9331770-4-7

Other Books by Atriad Press:

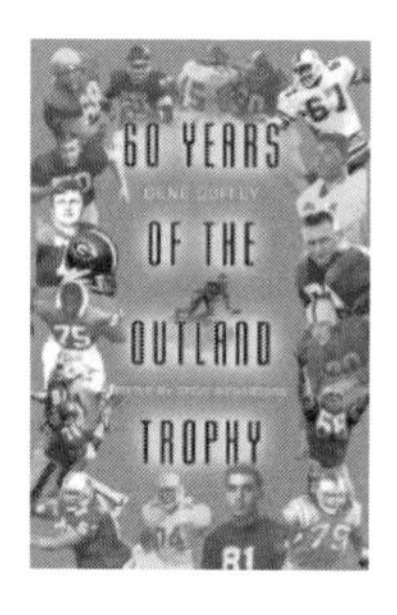

60 Years Of The Outland Trophy
by Gene Duffey
edited by Steve Richardson

ISBN 978-1-933177-08-3

Atriad Press books are available at your local bookstores nationwide and online at amazon.com &

www.atriadpress.com

or by contacting:

Atriad Press
13820 Methuen Green
Dallas, TX 75240

(972) 671-0002